Miriam Windham
Dec. '92

Keep Talking

CAMBRIDGE HANDBOOKS FOR LANGUAGE TEACHERS
General Editor: Michael Swan

This is a series of practical guides for teachers of English and other languages. Illustrative examples are usually drawn from the field of English as a foreign or second language, but the ideas and techniques described can equally well be used in the teaching of any language.

In this series:

Drama Techniques in Language Learning – A resource book of communication activities for language teachers
by Alan Maley and Alan Duff

Games for Language Learning
by Andrew Wright, David Betteridge and Michael Buckby

Discussions that Work – Task-centred fluency practice *by Penny Ur*

Once Upon a Time – Using stories in the language classroom
by John Morgan and Mario Rinvolucri

Teaching Listening Comprehension *by Penny Ur*

Keep Talking – Communicative fluency activities for language teaching
by Friederike Klippel

Working with Words – A guide to teaching and learning vocabulary
by Ruth Gairns and Stuart Redman

Learner English – A teacher's guide to interference and other problems
edited by Michael Swan and Bernard Smith

Testing Spoken Language – A handbook of oral testing techniques
by Nic Underhill

Literature in the Language Classroom – A resource book of ideas and activities *by Joanne Collie and Stephen Slater*

Dictation – New methods, new possibilities
by Paul Davis and Mario Rinvolucri

Grammar Practice Activities – A practical guide for teachers *by Penny Ur*

Testing for Language Teachers *by Arthur Hughes*

The Inward Ear – Poetry in the language classroom
by Alan Maley and Alan Duff

Pictures for Language Learning *by Andrew Wright*

Keep Talking

Communicative fluency activities for language teaching

Friederike Klippel

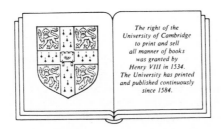

The right of the
University of Cambridge
to print and sell
all manner of books
was granted by
Henry VIII in 1534.
The University has printed
and published continuously
since 1584.

Cambridge University Press
Cambridge
New York   Port Chester
Melbourne   Sydney

Published by the Press Syndicate of the University of Cambridge
The Pitt Building, Trumpington Street, Cambridge CB2 1RP
40 West 20th Street, New York, NY 10011-4211, USA
10 Stamford Road, Oakleigh, Victoria 3166, Australia

© Verlag Lambert Lensing GmbH, Dortmund 1983
This translation © Cambridge University Press 1984

This edition first published 1984
Ninth printing 1991

Printed in Great Britain
at The Bath Press, Avon

Library of Congress catalogue card number: 48–9487

British Library cataloguing in publication data

Klippel, Friederike

Keep talking. – (Cambridge handbooks for
language teachers)
1. English language – Spoken English –
Study and teaching – Foreign speakers –
Problems, exercises, etc.
I. Title
428.3'4'076   PE1128.A2

ISBN 0 521 27871 6

Contents

121588

Acknowledgements

My sincere thanks are due to John Rogers of the English Language Institute in Wellington who convinced me that foreign language teaching should be a lot more than just grammar and word acquisition; to Graham Cass and Laurence Kane who were always willing to share their own teaching experience; to my students who never refused to try out yet another activity I had thought up; to Gordon Parsons and Ingrid Preedy who read parts of the final draft and suggested improvements; to Ilse Heitkamp who typed all the versions of the manuscript; to Michael Swan, Alison Baxter and Alison Silver at Cambridge University Press, who looked after and polished the English edition. Still, I could not very well have written this book if my family had not been helpful and understanding throughout – therefore my heartfelt thanks go to Dieter, Tina and Anne.

Friederike Klippel

The author and publishers are grateful to the authors, publishers and others who have given permission for the use of copyright material identified in the text. It has not been possible to identify the sources of all the material used and in such cases the publishers would welcome information from copyright owners.

Christiane Charillon, Paris for the drawings by Sempé on p. 150; Purnell Books for the extract on p. 167 from Michael Bond's *Book of Bears*.

Artwork by Lynn Breeze (pp. 148 and 149), Chris Evans (pp. 152, 178 and 179), Leslie Marshall (pp. 144 and 145), David Mostyn (pp. 146 and 147) and Wenham Arts.

Part 1

1 Introduction

> For the reader who is in a hurry: if you have just picked up
> this book in order to get some ideas for your classes
> tomorrow morning, start with 'Selection of activities' (p. 10).
> Then pick out one or two activities and read 'Using the
> activities' (p. 10). Once you have tried something out you
> may be interested in the rest of the introductory section.

1.1 What the book contains

For many years I have been teaching English as a foreign
language to different age groups and at various levels of
proficiency. Most of the activities in this book have been
developed in the last five years and tried out in several
versions, and the form in which they are described here is
certainly not a final one. Activities have to be adapted with a
group of learners in mind and I hope that teachers will feel
confident enough to make changes so as to suit the needs of
their particular groups of students.

Activities are invented, but we rarely know who invented
them. Like games or folk songs they are handed on from
teacher to teacher. One instance where the original idea can
be traced is the paper by Aronson et al (1975), which led to a
profusion of jigsaw exercises (see section 2.4). It has
happened quite frequently, though, that I have found
activities described elsewhere which I thought I had invented.
I have provided sources for all activities where other people's
work should be acknowledged.

The activities have been grouped in 13 sections, according
to type. Since some types of activity share certain
characteristics, there is some overlap. But as this book is
meant to be a source book for teachers and not a coherent set
of exercises, I feel this is a minor drawback. The 13 sections
have been arranged under three headings: 'Questions and
answers', 'Discussions and decisions', and 'Stories and
scenes'. Thus there is a kind of progression from relatively

1

simple exercises like interviews, which contain predictable structures, to more complex ones like role play or problem-solving activities. One cannot say, however, that an activity towards the end of the book is automatically more difficult than one towards the beginning.

All 13 sections are structured in a similar way. The introduction contains information on the kind of activity in question, and its possible uses in relation to specific language or educational aims. There are also ideas for the combination of different exercises, cross references and suggestions for further reading. Before this introduction, all the activities in the section are listed in a table and characterised briefly under the headings *topic type, level, organisation, preparation, time in minutes*.

Topic type   In this column one can see whether the activity is geared towards an exchange of personal information either on a more superficial (*pers.*) or a more intimate (*pers.**) level; whether it has a factual topic (*fact.*); or lastly whether it contains a fictitious element (*fict.*), which means that the participants have to invent stories or roles.

Level   The level indicated for each activity denotes the minimum language requirements for that activity. Thus an activity marked *beg.* (beginner's level) is suitable not only for beginners but also for students from beginner's level upwards.

Organisation   The following categories are used: *class* i.e. the whole class works together; *teams* i.e. two teams of equal size are formed; *groups* i.e. small groups of up to eight members each are necessary (some activities require groups of a particular size); *pairs* i.e. two students work together; *indiv.* (individuals) i.e. each student works on his* own.

Preparation   Teachers can see whether they need to prepare anything (worksheets, arranging the tables and chairs, etc.) before the start of the activity. *No* indicates that no preparation is necessary. *Yes* means that something has to be done beforehand; the descriptions of the activities themselves include detailed instructions on what has to be prepared in each case. The third kind of entry to be found in this column is *Part 2*, which means that a worksheet for the

---

* Since the English pronoun system obliges me to choose between 'he' and 'she', I have referred to the student in the masculine and the teacher in the feminine throughout.

activity, to be copied by the teacher, is included in Part 2 of the book.

Time in minutes   This gives a rough idea of how long the activity takes if it is done in the way described with an average-sized class (15–25 students).

The main part of each section consists of detailed descriptions of the activities, including information on the language practised and the educational aims being pursued, as well as hints on modifying the procedure. The procedure itself is usually explained in several steps.

Part 2 contains worksheets for 47 activities; these activities have been indicated in all the tables. There is also an alphabetical list of all the activities (on p. 188) with notes on different aspects, i.e. materials, organisation, time, aims/task for each one. Indexes of the language practised and the level of the activities follow (on p. 193). A list of the speech acts needed for certain activities (on p. 194) concludes Part 2, together with the bibliography. The latter is not restricted to the titles of the books mentioned but also includes relevant publications where further ideas on communicative exercises can be found.

1.2 Some basic considerations

The 123 activities in this book do not constitute a graded programme which should be taught step by step. The book's main function lies in offering many different kinds of exercises to complement traditional foreign language lessons and make them more interesting and lively. I have been guided by several principles in developing and selecting the activities, and I would like to discuss these briefly in turn: message-oriented communication, learner-centred activities, active learning, cooperation and empathy.

The term *message-oriented communication* (in the German original 'mitteilungsbezogene Kommunikation') was coined by Black and Butzkamm (1977). They use it to refer to those rare and precious moments in foreign language teaching when the target language is actually used as a means of communication. A prime instance of this use is classroom discourse, i.e. getting things done in the lesson. Sometimes real communicative situations develop spontaneously, as in exchanging comments on last night's TV programme or someone's new haircut. The majority of ordinary language teaching situations before reaching an advanced level, however, are geared towards *language-oriented communication*, or what Rivers calls 'skill-getting': they make use of the foreign language mainly in structural exercises and predetermined responses by the learners.

Since foreign language teaching should help students achieve some kind of communicative skill in the foreign language, all situations in which real communication occurs naturally have to be taken advantage of and many more suitable ones have to be created.

Two devices help the teacher in making up communicative activities: information gap and opinion gap. Information-gap exercises force the participants to exchange information in order to find a solution (e.g. reconstitute a text, solve a puzzle, write a summary). Examples of information-gap exercises can be found in sections 2.3 Guessing games, 2.4 Jigsaw tasks and 3.5 Problem-solving activities. Opinion gaps are created by exercises incorporating controversial texts or ideas, which require the participants to describe and perhaps defend their views on these ideas. Another type of opinion-gap activity can be organised by letting the participants share their feelings about an experience they have in common. Opinion-gap activities of the first type are included in sections 3.1 Ranking exercises, 3.3 Values clarification techniques and 3.4 Thinking strategies; those of the second type are to be found in section 3.2 Discussion games. Differences of opinion can either be the focus of a discussion, as in activity No. 48 *Guide*, or an obstacle to be overcome so that a consensus can be reached (e.g. No. 73 *Awards*).

By applying the principles of information gap and opinion gap to suitable traditional exercises the teacher can change them into more challenging communicative situations. Thus the well-known procedure at beginner's level of having students describe each other's appearance is transformed into a communicative activity as soon as an element of guessing (information gap) is introduced (see No. 11 *Back to back*). However, not all exercises can be spruced up like this. Manipulative drills that have no real topic have to remain as they are. Information and opinion-gap exercises have to have some content worth talking about. Students do not want to discuss trivia; the interest which is aroused by the structure of the activity may be reduced or increased by the topic.

Many of the activities are concerned with *the learners*

themselves. Their feelings and ideas are the focal point of these exercises, around which a lot of their foreign language activity revolves. For learners who are studying English in a non-English-speaking setting it is very important to experience real communicative situations in which they learn to express their own views and attitudes, and in which they are taken seriously as people. Traditional textbook exercises – however necessary and useful they may be for pre-communicative grammar practice – do not as a rule forge a link between the learners and the foreign language in such a way that the learners identify with it. Meaningful activities on a personal level can be a step towards this identification, which improves performance and generates interest. And, of course, talking about something which affects them personally is eminently motivating for students.

Furthermore, learning a foreign language is not just a matter of memorising a different set of names for the things around us; it is also an educational experience. Since our language is closely linked with our personality and culture, why not use the process of acquiring a new language to gain further insights into our personality and culture? This does not mean that students of a foreign language should submit to psychological exercises or probing interviews, but simply that, for example, learning to talk about their likes and dislikes may bring about a greater awareness of their values and aims in life. A number of activities adapted from 'values' clarification' theory have been included with this purpose in mind (see section 3.3).

Learning is more effective if the learners are actively involved in the process. The degree of *learner activity* depends, among other things, on the type of material they are working on. The students' curiosity can be aroused by texts or pictures containing discrepancies or mistakes, or by missing or muddled information, and this curiosity leads to the wish to find out, to put right or to complete. Learner activity in a more literal sense of the word can also imply doing and making things; for example, producing a radio programme (as in No. 118) forces the students to read, write and talk in the foreign language as well as letting them 'play' with tape recorders, sound effects and music. Setting up an opinion poll in the classroom (as in No. 15) is a second, less ambitious vehicle for active learner participation; it makes students interview each other, it literally gets them out of their seats and – this is very important – it culminates in a final product which everybody has helped to produce. Further devices to make learners more active are games (see section 2.3 Guessing games), fun and imagination (e.g. No. 5 *Trademark*, No. 87 *Brainstorming*) and group puzzles (e.g. No. 102 *Friendly Biscuits Inc.*).

Activities for practising a foreign language have left the narrow path of purely structural and lexical training and have expanded into the fields of values education and personality building. The impact of foreign language learning on the shaping of the learner's personality is slowly being recognised. That is why foreign language teaching – just like many other subjects – plays an important part in education towards *cooperation* and *empathy*. As teachers we would like our students to be sensitive towards the feelings of others and share their worries and joys. A lot of teaching/learning situations, however, never get beyond a rational and fact-oriented stage. That is why it seems important to provide at least a few instances focusing on the sharing of feelings and ideas. Jigsaw tasks (see 2.4), in particular, demonstrate to the learners that cooperation is necessary. Many of the activities included in this book focus on the participants' personalities and help build an atmosphere of mutual understanding.

Quite an important factor in education towards cooperation is the teacher's attitude. If she favours a cooperative style of teaching generally and does not shy away from the greater workload connected with group work or projects, then the conditions for learning to cooperate are good. The atmosphere within a class or group can largely be determined by the teacher, who – quite often without being aware of it – sets the tone by choosing certain types of exercises and topics.

Although the psychological considerations outlined above have influenced the selection of the 123 activities they have never been the only decisive factor. Mostly it has been my intention to collect activities which are effective learning situations for a foreign language. Quite a number of exercises have been rejected because the resultant language practice in no way justified the amount of time and preparation involved, even though they might have been excellent human relations or warming-up exercises. Since communicative aims are central to these activities they should not be used merely as fillers or frills on the odd Friday afternoon, but should have their place in revision or transfer lessons. Many types of language functions and structures can be practised in a new way. To my mind, however, it is far more important that the activities train the students to use their knowledge of the foreign language flexibly. They have to get their meaning across in order to do the exercise and will need to utilise every scrap of skill and knowledge they possess. Fostering this flexibility in the foreign language seems to me just as vital as trying to prepare for all communicative situations that may arise.

1.3 How to use the activities

This section deals with the importance of the atmosphere within the class or group, the teacher's role, and ways of organising discussions, as well as giving hints on the selection and use of the activities in class.

Atmosphere

Many of the activities in this book are focused on the individual learner. Students are asked to tell the others about their feelings, likes or dislikes. They are also asked to judge their own feelings and let themselves be interviewed by others. Speaking about oneself is not something that everyone does with ease. It becomes impossible, even for the most extrovert person, if the atmosphere in the group is hostile and the learner concerned is afraid of being ridiculed or mocked. The first essential requirement for the use of learner-centred activities (they are marked *pers.* in all the tables) is a relaxed and friendly atmosphere in the group. Only then can the aims of these activities be achieved: cooperation and the growth of understanding.

Groups or classes that have just been formed or are being taught by a new teacher may not develop this pleasant kind of group feeling immediately. In that case activities dealing with very personal topics should be avoided. The teacher may stimulate a good atmosphere by introducing both warming-up exercises (see 2.1) and jigsaw tasks (see 2.4). Even in a class where the students know each other well, certain activities may take on threatening features for individual students. In order to avoid any kind of embarrassment or ill feeling, the teacher should say that anyone may refuse to answer a personal question without having to give any reason or explanation. The class have to accept this refusal without discussion or comment. Although I have tried to steer clear of threatening activities, there may still be a few which fall into this category for very shy students. In any case teachers should be able to select activities which their students will feel at ease with. As a rough guideline teachers might ask themselves whether they would be prepared to participate fully in the activity themselves.

The teacher's role

A lot of the activities will run themselves as soon as they get under way. The teacher then has to decide whether to join in the activity as an equal member (this may sometimes be unavoidable for pair work in classes with an odd number of students) or remain in the background to help and observe. The first alternative has a number of advantages: for example the psychological distance between teacher and students may be reduced when students get to know their teacher better. Of course, the teacher has to refrain from continually correcting the students or using her greater skill in the foreign language to her advantage. If the teacher joins in the activity, she will then no longer be able to judge independently and give advice and help to other groups, which is the teacher's major role if she does not participate directly. A further advantage of non-participation is that the teacher may unobtrusively observe the performance of several students in the foreign language and note common mistakes for revision at a later stage. A few activities, mainly jigsaw tasks, require the teacher to withdraw completely from the scene.

Whatever method is chosen, the teacher should be careful not to correct students' errors too frequently. Being interrupted and corrected makes the students hesitant and insecure in their speech when they should really be practising communication. It seems far better for the teacher to use the activities for observation and to help only when help is demanded by the students themselves; even then they should be encouraged to overcome their difficulties by finding alternative ways of expressing what they want to say. There is a list of speech acts which may be needed for the activities (on p. 194) and the relevant section may be duplicated and given as handouts to help the students.

Ways of organising discussion groups

A number of different ways of setting up the communicative activities in this book are explained in the description of the activities themselves. For teachers who would like to change their procedures for handling classroom discussions (e.g. in connection with topical texts) a few major types are described below:

Buzz groups (see Cole 1970) A problem is discussed in small groups for a few minutes before views or solutions are reported to the whole class.

Hearing 'Experts' discuss a topical question and may be interviewed by a panel of students who then have to make a decision about that question.

Fishbowl All the members of the class sit in a big circle. In the middle of the circle there are five chairs. Three are occupied by students whose views (preferably controversial) on the topic or question are known beforehand. These three start the discussion. They may be joined by one or two students presenting yet another view. Students from the outer circle may also replace speakers in the inner circle by tapping them on the shoulder if they feel confident that they can present the case better.

Network The class is divided into groups which should not have more than 10 students each. Each group receives a ball of string. Whoever is speaking on the topic chosen holds the ball of string. When the speaker has finished he gives the ball of string to the next speaker, but holds on to the string. In this way a web of string develops, showing who talked the most and who the least.

Onion The class is divided into two equal groups. As many chairs as there are students are arranged in a double circle, with the chairs in the outer circle facing inwards and those of the inner circle facing outwards. Thus each member of the inner circle sits facing a student in the outer circle. After a few minutes of discussion all the students in the outer circle move on one chair and now have a new partner to continue with.

Star Four to six small groups try and find a common view or solution. Each group elects a speaker who remains in the group but enters into discussion with the speakers of the other groups.

Market All the students walk about the room; each talks to several others.

Opinion vote   Each student receives voting cards with values from 1 to 5 (1 = agree completely, 5 = disagree completely). After the issue (which needs to be phrased as a statement) has been discussed for a while, each student votes, and the distribution of different opinions in the group can be seen at a glance.

Forced contribution   In order to make sure that all the members of the class or group give their views in the discussion, numbers are distributed which determine the order of speaking.

Selection of activities

Naturally there are several possibilities for picking the right activity, ranging from skimming through the whole book to opening it at random and taking the first one you see. Here are three suggestions:

1 Look at the table which lists all the activities in alphabetical order (p. 188) and think about which selection criterion applies to you most. If you need to revise particular elements of the language, have a look at the right-hand column ('aims/tasks'). If you are looking for an activity grouped in a special way (i.e. pairs, groups, etc.), then you should concentrate on the column marked 'organisation'. If you are interested in an activity which does not need any preparation, then check 'materials'. After you have found a number of likely choices, read the detailed descriptions and then decide.

2 Choose a section that sounds interesting to you. Read the introduction to the section and pick out one or more activities from the table.

3 You may be looking for an activity which is suitable for a particular level or practises a certain grammatical structure. In that case the 'language' and 'level' indexes (p. 193) will help you.

Using the activities

Once you have found a suitable activity for your class you should do the following:

1 Prepare your materials in sufficient quantity.

2 Read through the 'procedure' section and if necessary note down the main steps. Think about how you are going to

introduce the activity and whether your students will need any extra help.

3 Decide which role you are going to adopt (joining, helping, observing?) and stick to it throughout the activity.

4 Let the students give you feedback on the activity when it is finished.

5 Make a note of any problems arising as well as your own comments and those of your students. You can then modify the activity when you use it again.

2 Questions and answers

2.1 Warming-up exercises

Activity	Topic type	Level	Organis-ation	Prep-aration	Time in minutes
1 Names	pers./fact.	beg.	class	yes	5–10
2 Name circle	pers./fact.	beg.	class	no	5–10
3 Name tags	pers.	int.	indiv.	yes	10–15
4 Identity cards	pers./fact.	int.	pairs	Part 2	10–30
5 Trademark	pers.	int.	indiv.	yes	15–20
6 Three adjectives	pers.*	int.	indiv./class	no	10–15
7 Stem sentences	pers.	int.	indiv.	Part 2	15–20
8 Choosing pictures	pers.	beg./int.	indiv.	yes	15–20
9 Clusters	fact.	beg./int.	class	yes	15–30
10 Groupings	pers./fact.	beg./int.	class/groups	Part 2	5–10
11 Back to back	pers.	beg.	pairs	no	10–20
12 Similar and different	pers.*	int.	pairs	no	10–20

pers. = personal; pers.* = more intimate; fact. = factual; beg. = beginners; int. = intermediate; indiv. = individuals; groups = small groups; pairs = two people working together; class = everybody working together; Part 2 = material for the exercise is to be found in Part 2.

When people have to work together in a group it is advisable that they get to know each other a little at the beginning. Once they have talked to each other in an introductory exercise they will be less reluctant to cooperate in further activities. One of the pre-requisites of cooperation is knowing the other people's names. A second one is having some idea of what individual members of the group are interested in. One important use of warming-up exercises is with new classes at the beginning of a course or the school year. If you join in the activities and let the class know something about yourself, the students are more likely to accept you as a person and not just as a teacher. A second use of warming-up activities lies in getting students into the right mood before starting on some new project or task.

However, even warming-up activities may seem threatening to very shy students. In particular, exercises in which one person has to speak about himself in front of the whole class (e.g. No. 5 Trademark) belong in this category.

You can reduce the strain by reorganising the activity in such a way that the student concerned is questioned by the class, thus avoiding a monologue where the pressure is on one person only. Students often find pair work the least threatening because everybody is talking at the same time and they have only got one listener. Depending on the atmosphere in your classes, you may wish to modify whole-class exercises to include pair or group work.

A number of warming-up exercises, (e.g. No. 8 *Choosing pictures*, No. 9 *Clusters*, No. 10 *Groupings*, No. 11 *Back to back* and No. 12 *Similar and different*), are also suitable for light relief between periods of hard work. No. 10 *Groupings* contains a lot of ideas for dividing students into groups and can precede all types of group work.

Most of the warming-up exercises are suitable for beginners because they do not demand more than simple questions and answers. But the language content of the exercises can easily be adapted to a higher level of proficiency.

The following activities which are described in later sections can also serve as warming-up exercises: No. 13 *Self-directed interviews*, No. 20 *Most names*, No. 41 *Go and find out*, No. 42 *Find someone who . . .*, No. 75 *Four corners*. There are further suggestions in Moskowitz 1978.

1 Names

Aims	*Skills* – speaking
	Language – questions
	Other – getting to know each other's names
Level	Beginners
Organisation	Class
Preparation	As many small slips of paper as there are students
Time	5–10 minutes
Procedure	*Step 1:* Each student writes his full name on a piece of paper. All the papers are collected and redistributed so that everyone receives the name of a person he does not know.

Step 2: Everyone walks around the room and tries to find the person whose name he holds. Simple questions can be asked, e.g. 'Is your name . . .?' 'Are you . . .?'

Step 3: When everyone has found his partner, he introduces him to the group.

Variations *1:* No direct questions of the type 'Are you . . .?' may be asked. Students have to find out by asking, e.g. 'Have you got more than one first name?' 'Does your surname end with an "e"?' 'Are your initials F. K.?'

2: Step 3 is expanded. When everyone has found his partner, he asks him a few questions about his family, background, hobbies, etc. When he introduces him to the group, these are mentioned as well.

2 Name circle

Aims	*Skills* – speaking
	Language – statements (This is . . ., I'm . . ., That's . . .)
	Other – learning each other's names, memory
Level	Beginners
Organisation	Class sitting in a circle; maximum of 25 students
Preparation	(For variation 2: toy animal)
Time	5–10 minutes
Procedure	The teacher begins by giving her name. The student sitting to the left of the teacher continues by first pointing at the teacher and saying, 'This is Fred Smith/Mrs Henderson,' then at himself giving his own name. In this way everybody in the circle has to give the names of all the people sitting to their right before introducing themselves.
Variations	*1:* Those students whose names have been forgotten by the person whose turn it is, have to stand up. They may sit down again when their names have been recalled correctly.
	2: A toy animal can be used to relax the atmosphere. It is handed from one person to the next in the circle and likewise introduced each time.
	3: With more advanced learners more complex statements can be used, e.g. 'The girl with the green pullover is Jane. The boy with the glasses sitting next to her is Jim.'

3 Name tags

Aims	*Skills* – speaking
	Language – questions, giving reasons, expressing likes
	Other – getting to know each other
Level	Intermediate

Organisation	Individuals
Preparation	Sheets of stiff paper in different colours, scissors, thick felt pens, masking tape
Time	10–15 minutes
Procedure	*Step 1:* Students cut out name tags for themselves in the shapes and colours that they feel suit them best. They write their names on the tags, fix them to their clothes with masking tape and start walking around the room.

Step 2: For a few minutes all the students just walk around and look at each other's name tags. They then pick out somebody whose tag they find interesting and talk about the colour and shape of their tags. Each student should try and talk to at least five other students.

Variations   *1:* After each student has made his name tag, all tags are collected and redistributed at random. The students fix the 'wrong' tags to their clothes on the right side of their chests. Again the students circulate and try and find the owner of the tag they are wearing. The correct tags are then fixed on the left side and a short conversation about the shape and colour of the tag follows. According to the level of achievement in the class the types of questions can be varied.

2: 'Mystery name tags' are used instead of proper name tags. First of all the class agrees on the type of information that should be given on the name tags. (e.g.   1   first name(s),   2   surname,   3   marital status,   4   children, 5   pets,   6   hobbies,   7   pet hates,   8   favourite country,   9   where the person would like to be right now) Each student now draws/writes a 'mystery name tag', by encoding the information for these nine points in abbreviations or symbols.

Example:

4 Identity cards

Aims *Skills* – speaking (writing)
Language – questions about personal data
Other – introducing someone else to the group, getting to know each other

Level Intermediate
Organisation Pairs
Preparation As many identity cards as there are students (see Part 2)
Time 10–30 minutes
Procedure *Step 1:* The students are grouped in pairs (see No. 10 *Groupings* for ideas) and each of them receives a blank identity card.

Step 2: The two students in each pair now interview each other in order to fill in the blanks on the identity card.

Step 3: Each student introduces his partner to the class using the identity card as a memory aid.

Variations *1:* The paired interviews can be conducted without identity cards. Each student must find out those things from his partner which he thinks are important or interesting.

2: The task 'Find out five things about your partner that one could not learn just by looking' can be given before the interviewing starts.

3: Each student draws a portrait on the identity card. All the cards are exhibited on the classroom wall.

4: If these interviews are done at the beginning of a course or seminar a question about individual expectations can be added.

5: With a very simple identity card this activity is suitable for beginners as well. An appropriate card might look like this.

Example:

name:	three things I like:
family:	
hobbies:	three things I don't like:
something I'd like to do:	

5 Trademark

Aims	*Skills* – speaking *Language* – giving and asking for personal information, stating likes and dislikes *Other* – getting to know each other
Level	Intermediate
Organisation	Individuals
Preparation	Overhead projector and as many transparencies as there are students, watersoluble OHP pens (alternatively: pieces of A4 paper and felt pens)
Time	15–20 minutes
Procedure	*Step 1:* Each student receives a blank transparency and a pen. Students are asked to draw 'trademarks' for themselves which tell something about their personalities. *Step 2:* Taking turns each student places his transparency on the OHP and explains his 'trademark' to the group. The others may ask questions.
Variations	Instead of having each student explain his drawing, every drawing can be given a number and shown for a short time while students suggest whose trademark it could be.
Remarks	This activity can be used both in newly formed groups as an icebreaker and in groups which have been working together for a while.

6 Three adjectives

Aims	*Skills* – speaking *Language* – making conjectures, agreeing and disagreeing, giving reasons *Other* – getting to know each other better
Level	Intermediate
Organisation	Individuals, class
Preparation	None
Time	10–15 minutes
Procedure	*Step 1:* On a piece of paper each student writes down three adjectives which he feels describe himself. All the papers are collected. *Step 2:* The teacher (or a student) reads out the papers one after the other. With each set of adjectives the group speculates who wrote them. The student concerned should be free to remain anonymous.

17

Variations   This activity can also be used to assess the atmosphere in a group at a particular time. Then each student is asked to write down three adjectives which characterise his state of mind.

Remarks   It may be advisable to revise suitable adjectives beforehand. (An extensive list can be found in Moskowitz 1978, p. 242.) The following adjectives are likely to be known after two or three years of learning English:

active, alive, angry, awful, bad, beautiful, big, black, blond, blue, boring, brown, busy, careful, cheap, clean, clever, cold, dangerous, dark, dead, deep, difficult, dirty, easy, empty, exact, exciting, expensive, fair, famous, fantastic, far, fast, fat, fit, free, friendly, funny, golden, good, great, green, grey, happy, hard, high, hungry, ill, intelligent, interested, interesting, international, jealous, late, left, little, lonely, long, loud, lovely, lucky, nasty, near, neat, new, nice, noisy, nosy, old, open, orange, polite, poor, pretty, quick, quiet, ready, red, right, rough, rude, short, slow, small, special, strange, strong, stupid, sweet, tall, terrible, thick, thirsty, tiny, tired, unfair, unfriendly, unhappy, warm, weak, wet, white, wild, wrong, yellow, young.

7   Stem sentences

Aims   *Skills* – reading comprehension, writing, speaking
Language – basic grammatical structures, asking someone to do something
Other – getting to know each other better

Level   Intermediate

Organisation   Individuals

Preparation   One handout for each student (see Part 2)

Time   15–20 minutes

Procedure   *Step 1:* Each student receives a copy of the handout. He is asked to fill it in.

     Step 2: Individual students ask others to read out certain sentences. Students may refuse if they feel their answers are too personal. A short discussion with other members of the group sharing their ideas can follow.

Variations   *1:* All completed handouts are collected. Each handout is read out and its author guessed.

     2: The students put on their completed handouts like

name tags. Then they walk around the room and talk in pairs
or small groups about their views and feelings.

Remarks Students are allowed to refuse to fill in sentences.

8 Choosing pictures

Aims *Skills* – speaking
Language – giving reasons, expressing likes and dislikes
Other – fun
Level Beginners/intermediate
Organisation Individuals
Preparation Collect about three times as many different pictures (of
objects, people, scenery, etc.), as there are students
Time 15–20 minutes
Procedure *Step 1:* All the pictures are put on a table. Each student
chooses two: one picture of something he likes; one of
something he dislikes.
  Step 2: Each student shows the two pictures to the class
and explains why he likes or dislikes them.
Variations Other selection criteria can be used, e.g. choose a picture that
you have strong feelings about (positive or negative) and one
that leaves you cold.
Remarks Suitable pictures can be found in newspapers, magazines and
among one's own collection of snapshots.

9 Clusters

Aims *Skills* – listening comprehension
Language – understanding instructions
Other – cooperation, speed of reaction, relaxation, dividing a
class into groups
Level Beginners/intermediate
Organisation Class
Preparation A list of commands for the teacher; a radio or cassette
recorder for background music. The room should be cleared
of tables and chairs.
Time 15–30 minutes
Procedure *Step 1:* The students walk around the room while the music is
playing. As soon as the music is switched off the teacher gives
a command, e.g. 'Stand together in groups of five.' When the

students have sorted themselves into groups the music continues and everybody again walks around alone until the next command.

Possible commands: 'Shake hands with as many people as possible'; 'Form a group with people of roughly the same height'; 'Stand together in groups of four and agree on a song you want to sing'; 'Mime a scene with at least three other people'; 'Find people whose birthday is in the same month as yours.'

    Step 2: After about five to eight commands which involve everybody, the game can be finished off by calling out numbers, e.g. 'seven'. That means that separate groups of seven students have to be formed. Anyone who is not in a group of seven is out.

Remarks   Step 2 is only suitable for younger students since it involves a lot of pushing and pulling.

10 Groupings

Aims   *Skills* – listening or reading comprehension, speaking
    Language – all elements
    Other – dividing a class into groups

Level   Beginners/intermediate

Organisation   Class, groups

Preparation   (see Part 2)

Time   5–10 minutes

Procedure   For many activities it is necessary to divide the whole class into pairs or groups. In some cases it is possible to let students find their own partners. For other exercises, however, it may be desirable for students who do not know each other well to work together or for different groupings to provide new stimuli. In these cases one of the following methods can be used. Since many of these incorporate the active use of the foreign language they are exercises in their own right, too. The procedure remains the same for all materials. Each student receives one item of information and has to find his partner(s) who hold(s) the remaining item(s).

1 Proverb matching (see Part 2, 10A)

Each student receives half a proverb card and has to find the student holding the other half. Together they have to think of a story/situation which illustrates their proverb, so that the others may guess the proverb.

2 Sentence matching (see Part 2, 10A)
3 Picture matching (see Part 2, 10B)
4 Mini-dialogues (see Part 2, 10C)
5 Word building
Six-letter words are scrambled and three letters written on each card. The two partners have to make up the word.

Examples: | mmr | | sue | | omh | | tde |

6 Film title matching

Examples: | HIGH | | NOON |

| AMERICAN | | GRAFFITI |

or: | WEST | | SIDE | | STORY | (for groups)

7 Personality matching

Examples: | WILLIAM | | SHAKESPEARE |

| ISAAC | | NEWTON |

| SHERLOCK | | HOLMES |

8. Word matching

Examples: | BUTTER | | FLY |

| BIRTH | | DAY |

| ICE | | CREAM |

9 Object matching (for groups)

Examples: | CAR | | LORRY | | BUS | | BICYCLE |

means of transport

| BOWL | | BASKET | | BOX | | BAG |

containers

Other possibilities are: pets, furniture, drinks, clothes, buildings, flowers, etc.

10 Country and product(s) matching

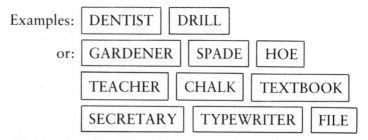

Examples: | ISRAEL | | GRAPEFRUIT |

or: | NEW ZEALAND | | KIWI | | LAMB |

Alternatively, capitals and flags may be added for the forming of groups.

11 Job and tool(s) matching

Examples: | DENTIST | | DRILL |

or: | GARDENER | | SPADE | | HOE |

| TEACHER | | CHALK | | TEXTBOOK |

| SECRETARY | | TYPEWRITER | | FILE |

12 Families (for groups)

Examples: | MR BAKER | | MRS BAKER |

| JIM BAKER | | JANET BAKER |

13 Numbers
Every player receives a number and the teacher announces number-groupings e.g. numbers 1, 3, 5 and 7 work together, etc.

There are innumerable further possibilities. Those mentioned here should give the teacher some ideas. Since the material used is not thrown away, the time spent preparing a few sets of pairing/grouping cards is time well spent.

11 Back to back

Aims   *Skills* – speaking, listening comprehension
Language – descriptive sentences (clothes, appearance), stating whether something is right or wrong
Other – observation, memory

Level	Beginners
Organisation	Pairs
Preparation	(Cassette recorder with music tape or radio)
Time	10–20 minutes
Procedure	*Step 1:* While the music is playing or the teacher is clapping, everybody walks around the room observing other people's clothes, hairstyle, etc. As soon as the music stops, each student pairs up with the person standing nearest and they stand back to back. Taking turns, each of them makes statements about the other's appearance, e.g. Student A: 'I think you're wearing blue jeans.' Student B: 'That's not right. My trousers are blue, but they aren't jeans' etc.
	Step 2: After a few minutes the music starts again and all partners separate. When the music stops a second time, the procedure described in Step 1 is repeated with a different partner. Three or four description phases are sufficient.
Variations	A student is allowed to keep making statements as long as they are correct. As soon as he mentions something that is wrong, it is his partner's turn to start describing him.

12 Similar and different

Aims	*Skills* – writing, speaking *Language* – making conjectures, expressing one's opinion, agreeing and disagreeing *Other* – getting to know someone else better
Level	Intermediate
Organisation	Pairs
Preparation	None
Time	10–20 minutes
Procedure	*Step 1:* The students work together in pairs. (For determining pairs, see ideas in No. 10 *Groupings*.) Each student writes down three ways in which he thinks that he and his partner are similar and three ways in which he thinks they are different. He does not show his partner what he has written.
	Step 2: First, both students tell each other about the similarities and talk about where they were right or wrong, then they talk about the differences.
Remarks	The points mentioned by the students may include obvious things like height or hair colour, as well as more personal characteristics like taste in clothes and behaviour in class.

2.2 Interviews

Activity	Topic type	Level	Organis- ation	Prep- aration	Time in minutes
13 Self-directed interviews	pers./fact.	int.	pairs	no	10–30
14 Group interview	pers./fact.	int.	groups	no	5–15
15 Opinion poll	fact./pers.	int.	groups	Part 2	30–45
16 Guided interviews	fact./pers.	int./adv.	pairs/groups	Part 2	15–25

pers. = personal; fact. = factual; int. = intermediate; adv. = advanced; groups = small groups; pairs = two people working together; Part 2 = material for the exercise is to be found in Part 2.

We watch, read and listen to interviews every day. In the media the famous and not so famous are interviewed on important issues and trivial subjects. For the advertising industry and market research institutes, interviews are a necessity. The success of an interview depends both on the skill of the interviewer, on her ability to ask the right kinds of questions, to insist and interpret, and on the willingness to talk on the part of the person being interviewed. Both partners in an interview should be good at listening so that a question-and-answer sequence develops into a conversation.

In the foreign language classroom interviews are useful not only because they force students to listen carefully but also because they are so versatile in their subject matter. As soon as beginners know the first structures for questions (e.g. Can you sing an English song? Have you got a car?) interviewing can begin. If everyone interviews his neighbour all students are practising the foreign language at the same time. When the learners have acquired a basic set of structures and vocabulary the interviews mentioned in this section can be used. A list of possible topics for further interviews is given at the end of the section. Of course, you may choose any topic you wish, taking them from recent news stories or texts read in class. In the warming-up phase of a course interviews could concentrate on more personal questions, as in No. 13 *Self-directed interviews*. An interview for a job is to be found in activity No. 117.

Before you use an interview in your class make sure that the students can use the necessary question-and-answer structures. A few sample sentences on the board may be a help for the less able. With advanced learners language functions like insisting and asking for confirmation (Did you mean that . . .? Do you really think that . . .? Did you say . . .?

But you said earlier that . . .), hesitating (Well, let me see . . .), contradicting and interrupting (Hold on a minute . . ., Can I just butt in here?) can be practised during interviews. When students report back on interviews they have done, they have to use reported speech.

Since the students' chances of asking a lot of questions are not very good in 'language-oriented' lessons, interviews are a good compensation. If you divide your class up into groups of three and let two students interview the third, then the time spent on practising questions is increased. As a rule students should make some notes on the questions they are going to ask and of the answers they get. If they write down all the questions in detail beforehand they have a questionnaire; several types of questionnaire are described in No. 15 *Opinion poll*. There is also a list of interview topics in No. 16 *Guided interviews*.

Interviews are contained in other activities as well, e.g. in No. 4 *Identity cards*, No. 45 *Question and answer cards*, No. 112 *TV interview*, No. 113 *Talk show*, No. 118 *Making a radio programme*. Some activities may be extended by interviews, particularly No. 65 *Futures* and all the activities in section 3.3 Values clarification techniques. Further suggestions for using interviews can be found in Dubin and Margol 1977, Krupar 1973, Revell 1979.

13 Self-directed interviews

Aims	*Skills* – writing, speaking
	Language – questions
	Other – getting to know each other or each other's points of view
Level	Intermediate
Organisation	Pairs
Preparation	None
Time	10–30 minutes
Procedure	*Step 1:* Each student writes down five to ten questions that he would like to be asked. The general context of these questions can be left open, or the questions can be restricted to areas such as personal likes and dislikes, opinions, information about one's personal life, etc.
	Step 2: The students choose partners, exchange question sheets and interview one another using these questions.

Step 3: It might be quite interesting to find out in a discussion with the whole class what kinds of questions were asked and why they were chosen.

Variations Instead of fully written-up questions each student specifies three to five topics he would like to be asked about, e.g. pop music, food, friends.

Remarks This activity helps to avoid embarrassment because nobody has to reveal thoughts and feelings he does not want to talk about.

14 Group interview

Aims	*Skills* – speaking
	Language – asking for and giving information
	Other – group interaction
Level	Intermediate
Organisation	Groups of four to six students
Preparation	None
Time	5–15 minutes
Procedure	In each group one student (who either volunteers or is drawn by lot) is questioned by all the other group members.
Variations	This activity is made more difficult and more interesting if the person interviewed is not allowed to answer truthfully. After the questioning the students should discuss how much these 'lies' revealed and how the students interviewed felt during the questioning.

15 Opinion poll

Aims	*Skills* – speaking, writing
	Language – making suggestions, arguing, agreeing and disagreeing, asking questions
	Other – planning and executing the solving of a task, cooperation, drawing up tables and lists, note taking
Level	Intermediate
Organisation	Groups of three to five students each (all groups should have the same number of students)
Preparation	Handouts for each group (see Part 2)
Time	30–45 minutes
Procedure	*Step 1:* The class is divided into groups of equal size. Each

group receives one topic in the opinion poll (see Part 2). The groups now follow the suggestions on the group card (Part 2) and agree on two or three questions they want to ask about their topic. Each group member prepares an interview sheet with these questions. He should fill in his own answers first.

Example:

NAME	FOOD	DRINK
1 Me	Cereal, toast and marmalade	Orange juice, 2 cups of coffee
2		
3		
4		
5		
6		

BREAKFAST

What do you usually have for breakfast?

Step 2: The groups are rearranged so that there is one member from each group in each new interview group. If there were six groups (e.g. breakfast, drinks, eating out, favourite dish, food hates, weight-watching) with five members each, then there are now five new groups which have six members each (one from each group). Each member of the new group has to get the answers to his questions from all the other members of the group. This means that in order to fill in his interview sheet each person has to talk to everybody else in the group.

Step 3: The orginal groups reassemble to organise their data. This may involve quite a lot of discussion where tables or diagrams have to be drawn.

Step 4: Each group presents their results either in the form of a short talk or by putting up lists, tables, etc. on the wall (or overhead projector), so that everybody can have a look.

Step 5: (optional) When everybody in the class has heard what the findings were, questions like 'Was there any result that surprised you?' 'What is the most important result?' 'How can we act on these results?' can be asked.

Variations   This procedure can be adapted to a great number of topics. Suggestions: Shopping, Travelling, Work, The Third World, Fun, Family life, Equality. Students can decide what sub-topics should be used for the group cards in a brainstorming session (see No. 87 *Brainstorming*).

Remarks   Students can work out their own questionnaires by using one of the following types of questions or stimuli.

Type A
Questions
about frequency   Choose the appropriate answer:

Example:
How often do you read a daily paper?

never	*rarely*	*sometimes*	*often*	*every day*
			×	

Type B
Statements   Choose degree of agreement:

Example:
Girls are more easily frightened than boys.

disagree strongly	*disagree somewhat*	*do not agree or disagree*	*agree some-what*	*agree strongly*
		×		

Type C Question/ statement   Choose one of the given answers/reactions:

Example:
You have just taken off from Heathrow airport, when the

○ You are pleased that women can become pilots at last.
○ You feel frightened.

Captain welcomes
you on board. The
Captain is a woman.

○ It does not bother you one way or
the other.
○ You write a letter of complaint to
the airline and tell them that you
will never fly with them again.

Type D
Yes/no
questions

Choose the appropriate answer:

Example:
Would you support
a strike in your firm?

yes	*no*	*don't know*

Type E Statements where blanks have to be filled in

Example:
Being a mother is the................ job in the world.

Type F Questions to be answered

Example:
Who do you think is going to be the next Prime Minister in
Britain?

16 Guided interviews

Aims	*Skills* – all four skills
	Language – all elements
	Other – imagination
Level	Intermediate/advanced
Organisation	Groups or pairs
Preparation	Handouts (see below and Part 2)
Time	15–25 minutes
Procedure	*Step 1:* Each group receives a handout (see below) of the answers and tries to work out the appropriate questions.
	Step 2: Solutions are read out.
Variations	Other types of guided interview can be developed by specifying the question forms that have to be used or the topics to be asked about. Some examples of interview-guiding worksheets for pair work are given in Part 2.

29

Interview

Here are 12 answers given in an interview. Think of questions that fit these answers and decide what the person who was interviewed is like.

1 Yes, I did.
2 This is quite true.
3 No. Gardening.
4 I can do either, but I prefer the first.
5 I can't answer that question.
6 Frogs and snakes.
7 New Zealand, Iceland or Malta.
8 As often as possible, but I'm not very good at it yet. I need to find someone to practise with.
9 I don't care which.
10 I wouldn't be able to tell one from the other.
11 Never.
12 That was the nicest thing that ever happened to me.

Interview topics

Smoking
Quality of life
Old and young under one roof
Single-parent families
Weather
Handicapped people
The best teacher I ever had
Keeping fit
The right to die
Illness
Minorities
Changing jobs
Moving house
Letter-writing
Favourite films
Eating out
Clothes
Plans and ambitions
Pets
Saving things
Old and new things
Private and public transport
Wildlife protection
Hunger
Loneliness

2.3 Guessing games

Activity	Topic type	Level	Organis-ation	Prep-aration	Time in minutes
17 What is it?	fact.	int.	class	Part 2	5–15
18 A day in the life	pers./fact.	int.	groups	no	15–20
19 Packing a suitcase	pers./fact.	int.	class	no	5–10
20 Most names	fact.	int.	indiv.	yes	15–25
21 Lie detector	pers.	int.	groups	no	10–15
22 Coffeepotting	fact.	beg./int.	groups	yes	10–15
23 What's in the box?	fact.	int.	pairs	yes	10–30
24 Definitions	fact.	int.	class/teams	yes	10–20
25 New rules	fact.	int.	groups	no	15–25
26 Hidden sentence	fact.	adv.	indiv./teams	yes	20–30

pers. = personal; fact. = factual; beg. = beginners; int. = intermediate; adv. = advanced; indiv. = individuals; groups = small groups; pairs = two people working together; teams = two large groups of equal size; class = everybody working together; Part 2 = material for the exercises is to be found in Part 2.

Everybody knows guessing games. It is not only children that like guessing; adults like guessing too, as shown by many popular TV programmes. The popularity of guessing games can be explained by their structure. Both chance and skill (in asking the right questions) play a part in finding the solution. The outcome of the game tends to be uncertain until the last moment, and so it is full of suspense. The basic rule of guessing games is eminently simple: one person knows something that another one wants to find out. How this is done is determined by an additional set of rules. These rules lay down, for example, the type and number of questions. The thing to be guessed differs greatly from game to game. It can be something one player is thinking of, an object seen only by one person, a word, an activity – or lots of other things.

As the person guessing has a real urge to find out something, guessing games are true communicative situations and as such are very important for foreign language learning. They are generally liked by students of all ages because they combine language practice with fun and excitement.

Before you try out a new guessing game with your class, make sure that the players know all the words and structures necessary for the game. If you are not sure, a trial run through the game may refresh your students' memories and show whether any revision is needed before you start playing in earnest. A trial run also has the advantage that the rules are demonstrated to all the players. Another element to be considered before playing is the organisation of the game, in order to guarantee that as many students as possible are actively participating most of the time. If you are playing a guessing game as a team contest it may be necessary to damp down the very competitive-minded. Games are a lot of fun even if they are not played in order to score points.

Variation is a vital ingredient of good games. You can try changing the rules of familiar games or doing things in a different order, and you will find that one game idea can be the nucleus of many new games.

If you cannot think of any new rules, have a look at collections of games for parties or children's groups. A lot of the ideas in those books can be transferred to foreign language teaching. There are also several publications devoted specially to foreign language teaching games (e.g. Chamberlin and Stenberg 1976, Lee 1979, Wright et al 1979). More theoretical books giving the rationale behind the use of games in foreign language teaching are by Rixon (1981) and Klippel (1980).

17 What is it?

Aims	*Skills* – speaking
	Language – questions, making conjectures, expressing uncertainty, giving reasons
	Other – fun
Level	Intermediate
Organisation	Class
Preparation	Transparencies for the overhead projector (see Part 2) with line drawings
Time	5–15 minutes
Procedure	The teacher puts a transparency with a complicated line drawing on the OHP. It should be out of focus (check position beforehand!), so that only a blurred image can be seen. The students guess what the drawing could represent, e.g. 'I think it could be a room.' 'I'm not quite sure, but the object on the left looks like a chair.' 'Is the round thing a lamp?' 'Perhaps the long shape is a person; it's got two legs.' etc.

Variations 1: Instead of home-made drawings, cartoons can be used (if a photocopier which prints onto plastic is available).

2: Instead of having the OHP out of focus, a sheet of cardboard with cut-out 'windows' at strategic points covers the picture. One 'window' after the other is 'opened'.

3: Points can be awarded not only for correct guesses but also for correct sentences.

18 A day in the life

Aims *Skills* – speaking, (writing)
Language – statements, asking about events (yes/no questions), simple past tense
Other – cooperation
Level Intermediate
Organisation Groups of four to six students each
Preparation None
Time 15–20 minutes
Procedure *Step 1:* The class is divided into groups. One member of each group leaves the room.

Step 2: The remaining group members decide on how the person who is outside spent the previous day. They draw up an exact time schedule from 8 a.m. to 8 p.m. and describe where the person was, what he did, who he talked to. So as not to make the guessing too difficult, the 'victim's' day should not be divided into more than six two-hour periods.

Step 3: The people who waited outside during Step 2 are called in and return to their groups. There they try and find out – by asking only yes/no questions – how the group thinks they spent the previous day.

Step 4 (optional): When each 'victim' has guessed his fictitious day, the group tries to find out what he really did.

19 Packing a suitcase

Aims *Skills* – speaking
Language – conditional
Other – imagination
Level Intermediate
Organisation Class versus two students

Preparation	None
Time	5–10 minutes
Procedure	*Step 1:* Two students are asked to leave the room. The rest of the class agrees on a person (either somebody from the class itself or a well-known person) for the two students to guess.

Step 2: The two students are called in again. They ask individual students what things (objects, qualities, characteristics) they would pack into the suitcase of the unidentified person, e.g. 'What object would you pack, Martin?' 'What positive quality would you pack, Susan?' The two students can discuss possible solutions together. They are allowed three guesses and must not take longer than three minutes.

Variations   *1:* The roles of questioning and answering could be changed so that the two students ask, e.g. 'Peter, would you pack a sense of humour?' (This way of playing the game would, however, reduce the amount of language practice for the class.)

2: The two students could agree on a person to be guessed by the class.

3: The game can be played as a competition in groups. One group thinks of the person to be guessed. The other groups have to discuss their questions and strategies, because they are only allowed one question or one guess per turn. The group which guesses correctly decides on the next mystery person.

20 Most names

Aims	*Skills* – speaking
	Language – yes/no questions
	Other – mixing in the class, group interaction
Level	Intermediate
Organisation	Individuals
Preparation	About three times as many name tags with the names of famous people written on them as there are students, masking tape (or safety pins)
Time	15–25 minutes
Procedure	*Step 1:* Without letting the student see it, the teacher fixes a name tag to each student's back.

Step 2: The students circulate around the room. They have to find out by asking yes/no questions 'who' they are. They

are not allowed to ask any one person more than three questions. As soon as somebody has found out who he is, he tells the teacher. If he is right he receives a new name tag. The student who has most names tags on his back – and thus has guessed 'his' different personalities most quickly in a given time (20 minutes) – is declared the winner.

Remarks   A list with suitable names is to be found in No. 54 *Personalities (1)*. Many more can be added, depending on the students' cultural background and who is in the news at the time.

21 Lie detector

Aims   *Skills* – speaking
Language – asking questions, giving reasons
Other – observation

Level   Intermediate

Organisation   Groups of six to seven students each

Preparation   None

Time   10–15 minutes

Procedure   *Step 1:* The students are divided into groups (see No. 10 *Groupings* for ideas). One member of each group leaves the room. In their absence the groups decide on a set of five to eight questions they want to ask the students. These can either be personal (e.g. 'What do you feel about corporal punishment?') or factual questions. In the case of factual questions the students asking them must not know the answers either.

Step 2: The students who went outside now return to their groups. They have to answer all questions, except one, truthfully; in one case they may lie. The rest of the group has to decide which answer was a lie. They have to give reasons to justify their opinion. The student tells them if they were right.

22 Coffeepotting

Aims   *Skills* – speaking
Language – questions, giving evasive answers
Other – fun

Level	Beginners/intermediate
Organisation	Two groups of different sizes (one group should have one third of the total number of students, the other, two thirds)
Preparation	Chairs arranged in two rows facing each other
Time	10–15 minutes
Procedure	*Step 1:* The groups sit down facing one another. Then the teacher, without letting the others see it, shows all the members of the smaller group a piece of paper with an activity (e.g. reading or skiing) written on it.

Step 2: The members of the bigger group now have to guess this activity. In their questions they use the substitute verb 'to coffeepot', e.g. 'Is coffeepotting fun in winter?' Both yes/no questions and wh-questions are allowed, but not the direct question 'What is coffeepotting?' The students in the smaller group are allowed to give evasive answers, though they should be basically correct. Each person in the smaller group is questioned by two members of the other group.

Step 3: As soon as a student from the guessing group thinks he has found the solution, he whispers it to the teacher and – if correct – joins the answering group. The game is finished when the original numbers of the groups (1/3 to 2/3) have been reversed.

23 What's in the box?

Aims	*Skills* – speaking
	Language – questions, explaining the *use* of an object without knowing its name
	Other – fun, vocabulary building
Level	Intermediate
Organisation	Pairs
Preparation	As many small containers (cigar boxes, matchboxes, tobacco tins, etc.) as there are students; one little object (safety-pins, stamp, pencil-sharpener, etc.) inside each container
Time	10–30 minutes
Procedure	Each student works with a partner (see No. 10 *Groupings* for ideas). One student from each pair fetches a box and looks inside without letting his partner see what is in the box. The second student has to guess the object.

If you think the students don't know the names of the objects, a piece of paper with the name (and the pronunciation) written on it should also be placed in the box. When the first student is quite sure his partner has guessed the object correctly (by describing its function or appearance) he tells him the name. The second student then fetches a box and lets the other one guess.

24 Definitions

Aims	*Skills* – speaking
	Language – definitions, new words
	Other – imagination, vocabulary building
Level	Intermediate
Organisation	Class or teams (if there are more than 20)
Preparation	At least one dictionary (English–English)
Time	10–20 minutes
Procedure	*Step 1:* One student is asked to leave the room. The remaining students choose a word, whose meaning they do not know, from the dictionary. The word is written on the blackboard. Each of the students now thinks of a definition for the word, only one student memorising the dictionary definition.
	Step 2: The student is called back in. Having been shown the word he asks individual students for their definitions. He can also ask additional questions about the (fictitious) meaning of the word. When he has listened to all (or some) of the definitions he says which one he thinks is the correct one.
Variations	Several unknown words are chosen and their correct definitions presented in random order. Words and definitions have to be matched.
Remarks	Students can be made aware of derivations of certain words from other languages they know or from other words they have learnt.

25 New rules

Aims	*Skills* – speaking
	Language – questions, discussion skills
	Other – observation
Level	Intermediate
Organisation	Groups of five to seven students each
Preparation	None

Time 15–25 minutes

Procedure *Step 1:* The class is divided into groups. Each group agrees on a rule that has to be followed in subsequent group conversations, e.g. nobody is allowed to speak before he has scratched his head; questions addressed to one member of the group are always answered by the right-hand neighbour; nobody is allowed to use the words 'yes' and 'no'.

Step 2: The groups now send one of their members as a 'spy' to another group. Each group talks about a given topic, e.g. What I like about our town. The 'spies' can ask questions and participate in the general conversation in order to find out the rule of their new group. The group members react to the 'spy's' contributions only as long as he does not violate the new rule.

Step 3: As soon as a spy thinks that he has discovered the new rule he returns to his group, and another group member is dispatched as spy to a different group.

Step 4: After a given time (15 minutes) all spies return to their own groups. A general discussion follows about the difficulties of discovering the rules and of keeping to them.

26 Hidden sentence

Aims *Skills* – speaking, listening comprehension
Language – all elements
Other – free conversation, guiding the conversation towards certain topics

Level Advanced

Organisation Teams, individuals

Preparation Cards with sentences (as many as there are students), topic cards

Time 20–30 minutes

Procedure *Step 1:* Two teams are formed. Two students, one from each team, come and sit at the front of the class. Each student chooses a sentence card. They do not show their sentences to each other or to their teams.

Step 2: The teacher chooses a topic card and announces the topic. The two students start off a conversation with each other on this topic. They have to guide the conversation in such a way that they can use the sentence on their card in a suitable context without anybody noticing it. Both teams listen attentively and try to guess the 'hidden sentence' of the student from the other team. If they think they hear it, they shout 'Stop!' and repeat the sentence. If they are correct, they score a point. Each team is allowed to shout 'Stop!' twice during each round. The conversation continues until 3 (or 5) minutes are up. For the next round two new students from each team come to the front.

Scoring can be organised as follows:

Guessing hidden sentence correctly: 1 point

Use of hidden sentence by student without detection: 1 point

Failure to use sentence: minus 1 point

This means that each team can gain a maximum of 2 points in each round (if they detect the opponent's hidden sentence and if their own team member uses his sentence undetected).

Suggestions for sentences
I really think it's old-fashioned to get married.
But I like children.
I've never been to Tokyo.
My mother used to bake a cake every Sunday.
The most dangerous thing you can do in rush-hour traffic is ride a bike.
Bus fares have gone up again.
Modern art is fascinating, I think.
I hate spinach.

Suggestions for topics
Pollution
Watching TV
Family life
Travelling
Fashion
Keeping fit

2.4 Jigsaw tasks

Activity	Topic type	Level	Organis- ation	Prep- aration	Time in minutes
27 The same or different?	fact.	int.	class/pairs	Part 2	15–20
28 Twins	fact.	int.	pairs	Part 2	5–10
29 Partner puzzle	fact.	int.	pairs	Part 2	10–15
30 What are the differences?	fact.	int.	pairs	Part 2	5–10
31 Ordering	fact.	int.	pairs	Part 2	10–15
32 Town plan	fact.	int.	pairs	Part 2	10–15
33 Weekend trip	fact.	int./adv.	groups	Part 2	30–45
34 Strip story	fact.	int.	class	yes	15–30
35 Information search	fact.	int.	groups	Part 2	10–15
36 Messenger	fact.	int.	groups	yes	10–15
37 Jigsaw guessing	fact.	int.	groups	Part 2	5–15
38 Getting it together	fact.	int./adv.	groups	Part 2	20–45

fact. = factual; int. = intermediate; adv. = advanced; groups = small groups; pairs = two people working together; class = everybody working together; Part 2 = material for the exercises is to be found in Part 2.

Jigsaw tasks use the same basic principle as jigsaw puzzles with one exception. Whereas the player doing a jigsaw puzzle has all the pieces he needs in front of him, the participants in a jigsaw task have only one (or a few) piece(s) each. As in a puzzle the individual parts, which may be sentences from a story or factual text, or parts of a picture or comic strip, have to be fitted together to find the solution. In jigsaw tasks each participant is equally important, because each holds part of the solution. That is why jigsaw tasks are said to improve cooperation and mutual acceptance within the group (see Aronson et al 1975). Participants in jigsaw tasks have to do a lot of talking before they are able to fit the pieces together in the right way. It is obvious that this entails a large amount of practice in the foreign language, especially in language functions like suggesting, agreeing and disagreeing, determining sequence, etc. A modified form of jigsaw tasks is found in communicative exercises for pair work (e.g. No. 27 *The same or different?* and No. 30 *What are the differences?*) in which pictures have to be compared.

Jigsaw tasks practise two very different areas of skill in the foreign language. Firstly, the students have to understand the bits of information they are given (i.e. listening and/or reading comprehension) and describe them to the rest of the group. This makes them realise how important pronunciation and intonation are in making yourself understood. Secondly, the students have to organise the process of finding the solution; a lot of interactional language is needed here. Because the language elements required by jigsaw tasks are not available at beginners' level, this type of activity is best used with intermediate and more advanced students. In a number of jigsaw tasks in this section the participants have to give exact descriptions of scenes or objects (e.g. No. 29 *Partner puzzle* and No. 32 *Town plan*), so these exercises can be valuable for revising prepositions and adjectives.

Pair or group work is necessary for a number of jigsaw tasks. If your students have not yet been trained to use the foreign language amongst themselves in situations like these, there may be a few difficulties with monolingual groups when you start using jigsaw tasks. Some of these difficulties may be overcome if exercises designed for pair work are first done as team exercises so that necessary phrases can be practised.

The worksheets contained in Part 2 are also meant as stimuli for your own production of worksheets. Suitable drawings (e.g. for No. 30 *What are the differences?*) can be found in magazines. If you have a camera you can take photographs for jigsaw tasks, i.e. arrangements of a few objects with the positions changed in each picture. Textual material for strip stories can be taken from textbooks and text collections.

Some of the problem-solving activities (section 3.5) are also a kind of jigsaw task, namely No. 102 *Friendly Biscuits Inc.* and No. 103 *Baker Street*. Further suggestions for exercises of this type may be found in Byrne and Rixon 1979, Gibson 1975, Kimball and Palmer 1978, Nation 1977, Omaggio 1976, Stanford and Stanford 1969 and Thomas 1978.

27 The same or different?

Aims	*Skills* – speaking, listening comprehension
	Language – exact description
	Other – cooperation
Level	Intermediate
Organisation	Class, pairs
Preparation	One copy each of handout A for half the students, and one copy each of handout B for the other half (see Part 2)

Time	15–20 minutes
Procedure	*Step 1:* The class is divided into two groups of equal size and the chairs arranged in two circles, the inner circle facing outwards, the outer circle facing inwards, so that two students from opposite groups sit facing each other. All the students sitting in the inner circle receive handout A. All the students in the outer circle receive handout B. They must not show each other their handouts.
	Step 2: Each handout contains 18 small drawings; some are the same in A and B, and some are different. By describing the drawings to each other and asking questions the two students in each pair have to decide whether the drawing is the same or different, and mark it S or D. The student who has a cross next to the number of the drawing begins by describing it to his partner. After discussing three drawings all the students in the outer circle move to the chair on their left and continue with a new partner.
	Step 3: When all the drawings have been discussed, the teacher tells the class the answers.
Variations	The material can be varied in many ways. Instead of pictures, other things could be used, e.g. synonymous and non-synonymous sentences, symbolic drawings, words and drawings.
Remarks	(Idea from Nation 1977.)

28 Twins

Aims	*Skills* – speaking, listening comprehension
	Language – exact description of a picture
	Other – cooperation
Level	Intermediate
Organisation	Pairs
Preparation	One copy each of handout A for half the students, and one copy each of handout B for the other half (see Part 2)
Time	5–10 minutes
Procedure	Each student works with a partner (for ideas on how to select partners see No. 10 *Groupings*). One student in each pair receives a copy of handout A, the other a copy of handout B. They must not let their partners see their handouts. By describing their pictures to each other and asking questions, the students have to determine which picture out of their set corresponds with one on their partner's handout.

Remarks   If the teacher produces a number of cardboard folders which each contain a set of instructions and picture sheets (A and B) in separate envelopes, all the students can work on different tasks at the same time and exchange folders in order to work on more than one set.

29   Partner puzzle

Aims   *Skills* – speaking
Language – describing the position of puzzle pieces
Other – cooperation
Level   Intermediate
Organisation   Pairs
Preparation   As many copies of the picture in Part 2 as there are students. Half of the photocopies should be cut up as indicated and put into separate envelopes.
Time   10–15 minutes
Procedure   Each student works with a partner. One student in each pair receives the complete picture, which he must not show to his partner; the other student gets the puzzle pieces. The first student now has to tell the second how to arrange the pieces; neither is allowed to see what the other is doing.
Remarks   If the teacher produces a number of cardboard folders (or big envelopes) with different pictures prepared in this way, students can exchange their tasks after completion.

30   What are the differences?

Aims   *Skills* – speaking
Language – exact description of a picture
Other – cooperation
Level   Intermediate
Organisation   Pairs
Preparation   A copy each of picture A (see Part 2) for half the students, a copy each of picture B (see Part 2) for the other half
Time   5–10 minutes
Procedure   *Step 1:* Each student works with a partner. One student receives a copy of the original picture, the other a copy of the picture with minor alterations. By describing their pictures to

one another and asking questions they have to determine how many and what differences there are between them. They are not allowed to show their pictures to their partners.

Step 2: When they think they have found all the differences they compare pictures.

Remarks   If the teacher produces a number of cardboard folders (or big envelopes) with different pictures prepared in this way, students can exchange their tasks after completion. (Idea adapted from Byrne and Rixon 1979.)

31 Ordering

Aims   *Skills* – speaking
Language – describing situations/actions shown in pictures, making suggestions
Other – cooperation

Level   Intermediate

Organisation   Pairs

Preparation   A comic strip (or picture story) of at least four pictures is cut up, and the pictures pasted in random order on two pieces of paper, so that each sheet contains half the pictures (see Part 2). Half the students receive one set of pictures each, the other half, the other.

Time   10–15 minutes

Procedure   *Step 1:* The students work in pairs. Each partner has half the pictures from a comic strip. First, each student describes his pictures to his partner. They do not show each other their pictures.

Step 2: They decide on the content of the story and agree on a sequence for their total number of pictures. Finally, both picture sheets are compared and the solution discussed.

Remarks   If the teacher prepares a number of picture sequences in this way, students can exchange materials after completion of one task.

32 Town plan

Aims   *Skills* – speaking
Language – giving directions
Other – cooperation

Level	Intermediate
Organisation	Pairs
Preparation	One town plan in two versions giving different pieces of information (see Part 2)
Time	10–15 minutes
Procedure	*Step 1:* The students work in pairs. Each partner receives a copy of the town plan, version A for the first student, version B for the second. The students ask each other for information which is missing from their plan i.e. the names of some streets (A has to find London Road, Aston Street, Rat Lane, Pen Street, Cocoa Lane, Station Square and Fair Fields; B has to find Park Street, North Street, Nottingham Road, High Street, Milk Lane, Trent Crescent and River Drive) and the location of certain buildings and other places marked on the map (A has to find Rose Park, the Old Bridge and the Town Hall; B has to find the Post Office, the department store and Windon Common). They must describe the way to these places starting at the point indicated on the map.
	Step 2: Student A then writes in the names of eight more places, using the spaces indicated by the numbers 1 to 15, without letting his partner see where he has written them in (his partner has a list of the places). B does the same for his eight places, using numbers 16 to 30. The partners then have to find out which numbers refer to which places by asking for directions, e.g. A: 'How do I get to the Chinese restaurant?' B: 'You walk up Linklow Hill and turn right into Ink Street. The restaurant is down the street on your left.'
Variations	Step 2 can be rendered more difficult if the partners do not use the starting point but describe the way from one place to another (e.g. from the bus station to the pub) without revealing the exact location of their starting point. This has to be deduced from the street names given.

33 Weekend trip

Aims	*Skills* – speaking
	Language – making suggestions, asking for and giving information, agreeing and disagreeing, expressing likes and dislikes
	Other – cooperation, finding a compromise

45

Level	Intermediate/advanced
Organisation	Groups of six to eight students
Preparation	Each group receives several copies of the map and a set of information cards (see Part 2)
Time	30–45 minutes
Procedure	*Step 1:* The first task of each group is to collect all the information and mark it (where necessary) on the master copy of the map. Either the members of each group come forward and report on individual points mentioned on their information cards, or they are questioned in turn.
	Step 2: The groups now have to work out a timetable and itinerary for a weekend trip into the area shown by the map. They are told: 'It is Friday afternoon (5 p.m.) and you have just arrived at Beachton. You are staying the night at a small hotel. Your landlady would like to know as soon as possible whether you will stay on for Saturday and Sunday night. Work out a jointly-agreed plan for the weekend (till Monday morning, when you have to leave Beachton at 10 a.m.). Decide where you would like to go, where you would like to stay, and what you would like to do and see.'
	Step 3: Each group presents its plan for the weekend trip.
Variations	*1:* The task can be varied by imposing a number of different constraints, e.g.
	– People are not allowed to spend more than a certain amount of money (information cards with fares, prices of accommodation and tickets, etc. need to be prepared).
	– Certain places have to be visited (the map is divided into four squares and places in three of them have to be included in the itinerary).
	– Only certain types of transport may be used in combination with particular types of accommodation (e.g. bicycle – youth hostel, train/bus – hotel, car – bed and breakfast, walking – camping).
	2: The trip need not be planned so as to satisfy all members of the group, which may break up into sub-groups (of at least two).
	3: Each group can work out suggestions for weekend trips (including transport, accommodation and prices) to be offered to the other groups, who have to choose.
Remarks	The map can be used for a lot of other language activities, like planning school bus routes, deciding on the location of a holiday camp/car factory/nature reserve, writing a tourist brochure, planning a motorway, etc.

34 Strip story

Aims   *Skills* – speaking
             Language – making suggestions, expressing one's opinion,
             asking for confirmation
             Other – cooperation
Level   Intermediate
Organisation Class
Preparation A story with as many sentences as there are students. Each
             sentence is written on a separate strip of paper.
Time   15–30 minutes
Procedure   *Step 1:* Each student receives a strip of paper with one
             sentence on it. He is asked not to show his sentence to
             anybody else but to memorise it within two minutes. After
             two minutes all the strips of paper are collected in again.
             Step 2: The teacher briefly explains the task: 'All the
             sentences you have learnt make up a story. Work out the
             correct sequence without writing anything down.' From now
             on the teacher should refuse to answer any questions or give
             any help.
             Step 3: The students present the sequence they have arrived
             at. A discussion follows on how everybody felt during this
             exercise.
Variations *1:* Instead of a prose text a dialogue is used.
             2: The task in this case involves the solution of a puzzle for
             which each student holds a vital piece of information.
Remarks   (See Gibson 1975.)

35 Information search

Aims   *Skills* – speaking, listening comprehension
             Language – asking for and giving information, making
             conjectures, saying that something is right or wrong, agreeing
             and disagreeing
             Other – cooperation
Level   Intermediate
Organisation Groups of six to eight students
Preparation Information cards which contain different pieces of
             information, one card per student (see Part 2), and one
             question card per group
Time   10–15 minutes

Procedure   *Step 1:* Each group receives a set of cards (as many
information cards as there are students, and one question
card). Tell the students that their task is to find out what
'plogs' are by sharing information, but that some of the
information they have been given is false. One person in the
group reads out the question from the question card. Then
they share the pieces of information on their information
cards.
Step 2: By comparing the statements on the cards they try
to pick out the pieces of false information, and write these on
a separate piece of paper. Then they discuss possible
solutions.

Remarks   If the teacher prepares different sets of material similar to that
presented in Part 2, groups can exchange tasks after
completion of the first one.

36 Messenger

Aims   Skills – speaking, listening comprehension
Language – describing something exactly
Other – cooperation

Level   Intermediate

Organisation   Groups of three to four students

Preparation   Lego bricks (one set of material for the teacher and one for
each group)

Time   10–15 minutes

Procedure   *Step 1:* Before the class starts the teacher builds something
out of Lego bricks and covers it with a cloth. When groups
have been formed and building materials have been
distributed, each group sends a messenger to look at the
'thing' the teacher has built.
Step 2: Each messenger reports back to his group and tells
them how to go about building the same thing. The
messengers are not allowed to touch the Lego bricks or to
demonstrate how it should be done. The group can send the
messenger to have a second look at the teacher's object.
When all the copies are finished they are compared with the
original.

Variations   Instead of Lego bricks, arrangements of tangram pieces or
other objects and drawings can be used.

37 Jigsaw guessing

Aims	*Skills* – speaking

Aims *Skills* – speaking
Language – making suggestions
Other – fun, cooperation

Level Intermediate

Organisation Groups

Preparation One puzzle for each group, the solution to which makes a word (see Part 2)

Time 5–15 minutes

Procedure *Step 1:* Each group receives a piece of paper with questions on it. The solution to each question is a word.

Step 2: All the students in the group try to make a new word out of the first letters of the individual words they have found.

Step 3: As soon as the group words have been formed, they are written on the blackboard. The first letters of all the group words give the solution to the whole puzzle.

Remarks The puzzles in Part 2 are designed for seven groups of four students each. The group solutions are 1: YEAR (Yawn, Eat, Accident, Ride); 2: APPLE (Afternoon, Pear, Postman, Like, Elephant); 3: DESK (Dear, Eleven, Song, Knife); 4: INTO (Indian, Name, Tea, Old); 5: LAMP (Love, Answer, Moon, Pen); 6: OVER (Orange, Valley, End, Rich); 7: HAND (Happy, Australia, New, Difficult).
The first letters of the group words form HOLIDAY (read backwards from group 7 to 1).

38 Getting it together

Aims *Skills* – speaking
Language – discussing, reporting on something, describing one's feelings
Other – cooperation, seeing a problem as a whole

Level Intermediate/advanced

Organisation Groups of five students

Preparation One envelope with three cardboard pieces per student (see Part 2; all the A pieces should be in one envelope, all the B pieces in another, etc.)

Time 20–45 minutes

Procedure *Step 1:* Each student receives an envelope. In each group there should be one envelope marked A, one B, one C, one D and one E. At a given signal, each student takes out his pieces. The aim of the group is to form five cardboard squares of exactly the same size. Each student may pass a piece of card to another person but he may not reach out and take one. No talking or any kind of communication is allowed during this phase. A student may refuse to take a piece of card which is given to him.

Step 2: These five squares can be made from the pieces:

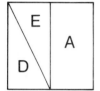 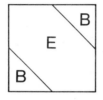

As soon as a group runs into serious difficulties or as soon as some squares have been formed, the teacher stops the exercise and asks the students to report what happened in their groups. She should encourage students to talk about their feelings, about their urge to communicate.

Variations The class can be divided into players and observers, so that a few groups of five students do the exercise, while others try to observe their behaviour. This may help the discussion later on.

Remarks A large part of this exercise does not involve talking or any kind of communication at all. The discussion, however, is usually very stimulating and intensive. Since both cooperation and communication – issues stressed in this book – are central to the exercise, it seems right to include it. (See *Learning for Change* 1977.)

2.5 Questioning activities

Activity	Topic type	Level	Organis-ation	Prep-aration	Time in minutes
39 What would happen if . . .?	fact.	int.	class	yes	10–15
40 Question game	fact./pers.	int.	groups	Part 2	15–30
41 Go and find out	fact./pers.	int.	indiv./class	Part 2	15–30
42 Find someone who . . .	fact./pers.	int.	indiv./class	Part 2	10–20
43 Something else	pers.*	int.	indiv./groups	no	10–20
44 Ageless	pers.*	int.	groups/class	yes	10–20
45 Question and answer cards	fact.	int.	pairs	Part 2	10–15

pers. = personal; pers.* = more intimate; fact. = factual; int. = intermediate;
indiv. = individuals; groups = small groups; pairs = two people working together;
class = everybody working together; Part 2 = material for the exercises is to be found in Part 2.

This last section in the chapter is something of a mixed bag, in so far as it contains all those activities which, although they centre around questioning, do not fit into any of the previous sections. First of all there are humanistic exercises (No. 43 *Something else* and No. 44 *Ageless*) that focus on the learners themselves, their attitudes and values. Secondly there is a kind of exercise that could be employed to teach learners about the cultural background of the target country (No. 45 *Question and answer cards*). Thirdly there is a board game (No. 40 *Question game*). Last of all there are three activities suitable either as warming-up exercises or as strategies for tackling more factual topics. The worksheets belonging to these exercises (in Part 2) can be modified accordingly. Many of these activities are quite flexible, not only as regards their content but also in terms of procedure. By simply introducing a few new rules, e.g. a limit on the number of questions or a time-limit they are transformed into games.

As soon as students are able to produce yes/no and wh-questions most of these activities can be used. You may, however, have to adapt the worksheets as these are not always aimed at the earliest stage at which an exercise can be used. For reasons of motivation similar activities, like No. 41 *Go and find out* and No. 42 *Find someone who . . .*, should not be done directly one after the other.

For activities in which question forms are practised see sections 2.1 to 2.4. The book by Moskowitz (1978) contains a great number of humanistic exercises.

39   What would happen if . . .?

Aims	*Skills* – speaking
	Language – if-clauses, making conjectures, asking for confirmation
	Other – imagination
Level	Intermediate
Organisation	Class
Preparation	About twice as many slips of paper with an event/situation written on them as there are students
Time	10–15 minutes
Procedure	Every student receives one or two slips of paper with sentences like these on them: 'What would happen if a shop gave away its goods free every Wednesday?' 'What would you do if you won a trip for two to a city of your choice?' One student starts by reading out his question and then asks another student to answer it. The second student continues by answering or asking a third student to answer the first student's question. If he has answered the question he may then read out his own question for somebody else to answer. The activity is finished when all the questions have been read out and answered.
Variations	The students can prepare their own questions. Some more suggestions:

What would happen
   if everybody who told a lie turned green?
   if people could get a driving licence at 14?
   if girls had to do military service?
   if men were not allowed to become doctors or pilots?
   if children over 10 were allowed to vote?
   if gold was found in your area?
   if a film was made in your school/place of work?
   if headmasters had to be elected by teachers and pupils?
   if smoking was forbidden in public places?
   if the price of alcohol was raised by 300 per cent?

What would you do
   if you were invited to the Queen's garden party?
   if a photograph of yours won first prize at an exhibition?
   if your little sister aged 14 told you she was pregnant?
   if you saw your teacher picking apples from her neighbour's tree?
   if a salesman called at your house and tried to sell you a sauna bath?

if your horoscope warned you against travelling when you
want to go on holiday?
if it rained every day of your holiday?
if you got a love letter from somebody you did not know?
if you found a snake under your bed?
if you got lost on a walk in the woods?
if you were not able to remember numbers?
if somebody hit a small child very hard in your presence?
if you found a £20 note in a library book?
if your friend said she did not like the present you had
given her?
if you suddenly found out that you could become invisible
by eating spinach?
if you broke an expensive vase while you were baby-sitting
at a friend's house?
if you invited somebody to dinner at your house but they
forgot to come?
if you forgot you had asked four people to lunch and didn't
have any food in the house when they arrived?
if a young man came up to you, gave you a red rose and
said that you were the loveliest person he had seen for a
long time?
if you noticed that you hadn't got any money on you and
you had promised to ring your mother from a call box at
exactly this time?
if you could not sleep at night?

40 Question game

Aims	*Skills* – speaking, reading comprehension, listening comprehension *Language* – questions and answers *Other* – getting to know each other
Level	Intermediate
Organisation	Groups of six students
Preparation	Two dice of different colours, a question board (see Part 2) and 10 (or 15) question cards (see Part 2) for each group
Time	15–30 minutes
Procedure	*Step 1:* Each group receives the dice, question board and question cards. The question cards are put in piles face down next to the numbers 1 to 5 on the question board. Each student in the group is given a number from 1 to 6.

53

Step 2: Taking turns, each student throws the dice. One die indicates the question to be asked (the one on top of the pile of question cards next to the number thrown) the other, the person who must answer the question. If the 'question-die' shows a 6, the person whose turn it is may ask a question of the student whose number was thrown with the 'student-die'. The exercise is finished when everybody has answered every question.

Variations   1: Students can prepare different questions.

2: Instead of personal questions others concerning subjects or topics taught in class can be chosen.

41   Go and find out

Aims   *Skills* – speaking (writing)
Language – asking for and giving information
Other – getting to know each other, relaxation, losing inhibitions

Level   Intermediate

Organisation   Individuals, class

Preparation   A different task for each student (see Part 2), a list each of the names of all the students (in big classes)

Time   15–30 minutes

Procedure   Step 1: Each student receives a task and a list of the names of all the other students (in small groups where students know each other the list of names is not necessary).

Step 2: Each student now questions everybody else, according to his task. He writes the answers down, and crosses off the list the names of the people he has asked.

Step 3: When everybody has finished asking, each student reads out his question/task and reports his findings.

Variations   1: The types of task can be varied according to the background, age and interests of the group.

2: Two or three students can be given the same task.

Remarks   There is a similar exercise in No. 15 *Opinion poll.*

42   Find someone who . . .

Aims   *Skills* – speaking
Language – questions
Other – getting to know each other

Level	Intermediate
Organisation	Individuals, class
Preparation	Handout (see Part 2; it should contain roughly as many sentences as there are students)
Time	10–20 minutes
Procedure	*Step 1:* Each student receives a handout. Everyone walks around the room and questions other people about things on the handout. As soon as somebody finds another student who answers 'yes' to one of the questions, he writes his name in the space and goes on to question someone else, because each name may only be used once. If a student overhears somebody answering 'yes' to another person's question he is not allowed to use that name himself. After a given time (15 minutes) or when someone has filled in all the blanks, the questioning stops.
	Step 2: Students read out what they have found out. They can preface their report with: 'I was surprised that X liked . . .', 'I never thought that Y liked . . .'.

43 Something else

Aims	*Skills* – speaking
	Language – conditional
	Other – thinking about oneself, getting to know each other, imagination
Level	Intermediate
Organisation	Individuals or groups (in large classes)
Preparation	None
Time	10–20 minutes
Procedure	The teacher explains the basic idea of the activity: 'Suppose you weren't you but something else entirely, e.g. an animal or a musical instrument. Just think what you would like to be and why, when I tell you the categories.' Possible categories are: colours, days of the week, kinds of weather, musical instruments, months, countries, cities, articles of clothing, songs, kinds of fruit, flowers, kinds of literature, pieces of furniture, food, toys, etc.
Variations	*Something else* can also be played as a guessing game. Two students are asked to leave the room while the rest of the class agree on a person to be guessed. When the two students are called back in they ask questions such as: 'What would the person be if he or she was an animal? a colour? a building? a

landscape? a piece of music? a musical instrument? a flower?, etc. From the answers, characteristics of the person can be deduced and his or her identity guessed. If the person to be guessed is present he can comment on the comparisons made, e.g. 'I was surprised that . . ., I don't see myself as . . ., Being compared to . . . was quite startling/disappointing/ flattering/embarrassing . . .'

Remarks Since the insights gained in this activity can be quite unsettling for the people concerned, it should only be organised in groups which have a friendly, supportive atmosphere.
(Idea adapted from Moskowitz 1978.)

44 Ageless

Aims *Skills* – speaking
Language – questions about one's age and feelings about age
Other – talking and thinking about oneself

Level Intermediate

Organisation Groups or class (if not more than 15 students)

Preparation Questions about age, one list of questions for each group (see below)

Time 10–20 minutes

Procedure Each group/the class talks about age, guided by the following questions:
'What do you like about your present age? What did you like about being younger? What will you like about being 5/10/30 years older? What will you like about being elderly? What is the ideal age? Why? What could you say to someone who is not happy about his age? Do you often think about age/growing old/staying young? Does advertising influence your feelings?'

Variations The questions can be distributed to different students, who ask the other members of the class/their groups when it is their turn.

Remarks This exercise works well if the students have known each other for a while and a friendly, supportive atmosphere has been established.
(Idea adapted from Moskowitz 1978.)

45 Question and answer cards

Aims	*Skills* – speaking
	Language – formulating questions
	Other – learning something about English-speaking countries
Level	Intermediate
Organisation	Pairs
Preparation	One card per student (see Part 2)
Time	10–15 minutes
Procedure	The students work in pairs. They question each other in turn about the things specified on their cards. (If several cards have been distributed each pair of students exchanges cards with another after having answered all the questions.)
Variations	1: Each student receives a different card and has to find his partner before he can start with the questions.
	2: The students make up their own cards about subjects dealt with in class. For this they should use the second type of card (see Part 2), where answers are not given.
Remarks	Other examples for guided questioning are to be found in No. 16 *Guided interviews*.

3 Discussions and decisions

3.1 Ranking exercises

Activity	Topic type	Level	Organis- ation	Prep- aration	Time in minutes
46 Rank order	pers.	int./adv.	indiv.	Part 2	15–20
47 Qualities	pers./fact.	int.	indiv./groups/class	no	10–20
48 Guide	fact.	int./adv.	groups	Part 2	15–30
49 Priorities	pers./fact.	int./adv.	indiv./groups	Part 2	15–20
50 Desert island (1)	fact.	beg./int.	pairs/class	no	10–20
51 NASA game	fact.	int./adv.	indiv./pairs	Part 2	10–15
52 Values ladder	pers.	adv.	indiv.	no	15–20
53 Looking for a job	fact.	int./adv.	groups	Part 2	20–40
54 Personalities (1)	pers./fact.	beg.	indiv.	no	10–15
55 Guarantees	pers.	int./adv.	teams	yes	30–40
56 Good teacher	pers./fact.	int./adv.	indiv.	Part 2	15–20
57 Job prestige	pers./fact.	int./adv.	pairs	no	15–20

pers. = personal; fact. = factual; beg. = beginners; int. = intermediate; adv. = advanced; indiv. = individuals; groups = small groups; pairs = two people working together; teams = two large groups of equal size; class = everybody working together; Part 2 = material for the exercise is to be found in Part 2.

These exercises require students to put a certain number of items from a given list into an order of importance or preference. This rearranging phase is usually followed by a period of discussion, when students explain or defend their choices in pairs or small groups. The underlying situations, problems, or questions for these exercises are taken from widely different contexts, e.g. No. 47 *Qualities* motivates the students to consider various desirable characteristics for people in general, thus helping them clarify their own values. In ranking the items from No. 51 *NASA game*, however, personal values and prejudices play a relatively minor part, whereas common sense and general knowledge of the world are of greater importance. That is why correct solutions can only be given for exercises like this one which remain outside the purely subjective sphere. It is to be hoped that the discussion of personal rankings will lead some students to question their own decisions and increase their tolerance and understanding.

Ranking exercises practise interactive language, for instance agreeing, comparing, contradicting, disagreeing, giving reasons. As in some jigsaw tasks the students may experience a difference of opinion and may be stimulated to discuss these differences. Reluctant students can be made to discuss their lists in detail if they are asked to produce an integrated list of rankings for their group.

A variety of procedures for using ranking exercises can be suggested. The first step remains the same for all procedures: the students are made familiar with the task. This can be done either by oral presentation by the teacher or by giving the students handouts. Work on a ranking exercise can be continued in one of the following ways:

— Each student works on his own and writes down his solutions. These lists are then compared and discussed in pairs, in small groups or with the whole class.
— When each student has finished his list, the students sit down together in small groups and try to agree on a common listing, which has to be presented and defended in a final general discussion.
— Groups of increasing size (two members, then four, then eight) discuss the lists and aim for an agreed list at each stage.
— All students whose lists are similar work together in groups and try to find as many arguments as possible for their rank order. A final discussion with the whole class follows.

It is recommended that a time limit be fixed for the first step as students tend to vary considerably in the time they need for deciding on a ranking.

Ranking exercises are a kind of preliminary step for the less structured values clarification techniques in section 3.3 and, for inexperienced classes, should precede them.

Further suggestions for ranking exercises can be found in Howe and Howe 1975, Papalia 1976b, Rogers 1978, Simon et al 1972.

46 Rank order

Aims	*Skills* – reading comprehension, speaking *Language* – expressing likes and dislikes, giving reasons, expressing certainty and uncertainty *Other* – thinking about one's own values
Level	Intermediate/advanced
Organisation	Individuals (pairs and group work also possible)
Preparation	Handout (see Part 2)
Time	15–20 minutes
Procedure	*Step 1:* Each student receives a copy of the handout. He is asked to fill it in according to the instructions. It should be stressed that everybody is asked not only to state his first choice but to number all the choices in order of preference. (10 minutes) *Step 2:* When all the items have been ranked students share their results with their neighbour (in a large class) or with the whole class. Depending on the interests of the participants this step can lead to a discussion by individual members of the class of what is considered important.
Variations	If the questions suggested in Part 2 are considered to be too personal for a particular class, alternatives can easily be found, e.g. pollution, social problems, political attitudes, etc.
Remarks	Because of the personal nature of the questions selected for the handout it is very important to create a supportive and friendly atmosphere within the class. During Step 2 students should be encouraged to help each other accept themselves and become aware of their values rather than criticise or condemn each other's attitudes. It should be perfectly acceptable for a student to refuse to disclose his answer if he feels shy or insecure.

47 Qualities

Aims	*Skills* – speaking *Language* – describing personal qualities, stating preferences, asking for and giving reasons, contradicting; comparative and superlative *Other* – thinking about one's own values as regards other people
Level	Intermediate

Organisation	Individuals (Step 1), groups of three or four students (Step 2), whole class (Step 3)
Preparation	None
Time	10–20 minutes
Procedure	*Step 1:* The teacher presents the group with the following list, either writing it on the blackboard or the overhead projector, or distributing it as a handout:

    reliability
    being a good listener
    strength
    honesty
    intelligence
    generosity
    caution
    being funny
    stubbornness
    helpfulness

Each student should think about how important he considers each quality. He then rearranges the list in order of importance, starting with the most important quality.

    Step 2: Students sit together in small groups and talk about their ranking of the qualities. A group consensus should be aimed at.

    Step 3: The whole class aims to find a ranking order for the qualities which everyone agrees to (optional).

Variations	The same procedure can be followed for different lists, which have been adapted to group interests and the age of the students. Suggestions: reasons for wanting/keeping a pet, things to make a holiday worthwhile, qualities a good car should have, reasons for watching TV, qualities of good parents/friends/politicians/scientists/nurses/doctors, etc.

48 Guide

Aims	*Skills* – speaking
	Language – arguing, giving and asking for reasons, defending one's opinions, contradicting, making suggestions
	Other – cooperation
Level	Intermediate/advanced
Organisation	Groups of three to five students each (even number of groups)
Preparation	Handout (see Part 2)
Time	15–30 minutes

Procedure   *Step 1:* The class is divided into an even number of small groups. Half of these groups receive copies of the handout. The other half are presented orally with the same situation but have to find ten places without being given a list to choose from. Both kinds of group should reach an agreement after 10 to 15 minutes' discussion.

     Step 2: Each group elects a speaker who has to defend the solution arrived at by his group. All the speakers sit in the middle of the circle ('fishbowl' arrangement, see p. 9) and present their results in turn. In the ensuing discussion, they should attempt to reach a common solution to the choice of places (if not their sequence).

Variations   *1:* The same procedure can be adopted with all the groups receiving the handout and the same task.

     2: An intermediate step can be introduced to enable all groups working on the same task to discuss strategies for the 'fishbowl' phase.

     3: The handout can also be used in ways described in No. 46 *Rank order.*

Remarks   In multi-national groups it may be difficult to go beyond Step 1, in which case it may be more profitable to ask people from similar cultural backgrounds to work together and present their results to the whole class. Differences between solutions can then be discussed.

(Idea adapted from Rogers 1978.)

49 Priorities

Aims   *Skills* – reading comprehension, speaking
Language – giving and asking for reasons
Other – thinking about an everyday situation, preparing for general discussion of compulsory education

Level   Intermediate/advanced

Organisation   Individuals, groups of three to five members

Preparation   Handout (see Part 2; twice as many copies as there are students)

Time   15–20 minutes

Procedure   *Step 1:* Each student receives a copy of the handout and is asked to rank the items in order of importance from 1 to 12. The rank number for each item should be entered in both boxes. When everybody has finished (after about 5 minutes), all the strips marked *Check* are torn off and collected by the teacher. She calculates the total rank of each item by adding up all the rank numbers given. The item with the lowest number is considered the most important one by most students, the one with the highest number the least important.

    Step 2: Meanwhile the students are given another copy of the handout, and they sit down in small groups and attempt to find a common ranking for the items. Group results are then compared with the overall result of individual ranking.

Variations   *1:* Step 2 can be omitted and a general discussion can follow Step 1 directly.

    2: Other questions can be worked on in the same way.

50 Desert island (1)

Aims   *Skills* – speaking
Language – giving and asking for reasons, making suggestions, agreeing and disagreeing, if-clauses
Other – imagination, fun

Level   Beginners/intermediate
Organisation   Pairs, class
Preparation   None
Time   10–20 minutes
Procedure   *Step 1:* The teacher tells the class about the situation and sets the task:

'You are stranded on a desert island in the Pacific. All you have is the swim-suit and sandals you are wearing. There is food and water on the island but nothing else. Here is a list of things you may find useful. Choose the eight most useful items and rank them in order of usefulness.

a box of matches	ointment for cuts and burns
a magnifying glass	a saucepan
an axe	a knife and fork
a bottle of whisky	20 metres of nylon rope
an atlas	a blanket
some metal knitting-needles	a watch
a transistor radio with batteries	a towel
a nylon tent	a pencil and paper
a camera and five rolls of film	

Work with a partner. You have 8 minutes.'

Step 2: Students present their solutions and defend their choices against the others' arguments.

Variations *1:* To enhance the fantasy nature of the exercise, more exotic and apparently useless items can be chosen for the original list. This will force the students to find new ways of using items, e.g. a bottle can be used for posting letters, a mirror as a signalling device.

2: Other procedures, i.e. the 'star' method or the 'buzz group' system can be used instead of the two steps suggested here (see p. 9).

3: Students can be asked to provide material for other situations themselves, e.g. 'For a bet, you will have to spend three weeks in a lonely cottage on the Scottish moors completely on your own. Which six of these things would you like to take along and why?'

Remarks There is, of course, no correct solution to the task in this exercise. It should be seen as a lighthearted activity which will help provide an element of imagination and fun in the foreign language class.

51 NASA game

Aims *Skills* – speaking
Language – giving and asking for reasons, expressing certainty and uncertainty, making objections
Other – general knowledge
Level Intermediate/advanced
Organisation Individuals, pairs
Preparation Handout (see Part 2)
Time 10–15 minutes
Procedure *Step 1:* Each student is given the handout and asked to rank the 15 items. (Note that the moon has no atmosphere, so it is impossible to make fire or to transmit sound signals; the moon has no magnetic poles.)

Step 2: Each student then compares his solution with that of his neighbour and they try to arrive at a common ranking.

Step 3: The results of Step 2 are discussed and compared around the class.

Remarks (Idea adapted from Rogers 1978.)

52 Values ladder

Aims *Skills* – listening comprehension, speaking
Language – expressing personal insights and conjectures, giving reasons, simple past tense
Other – thinking about one's own spontaneous reactions, discovering personal values

Level Advanced

Organisation Individuals

Preparation None

Time 15–20 minutes

Procedure *Step 1:* The students are asked to draw a flight of nine steps on a piece of paper.

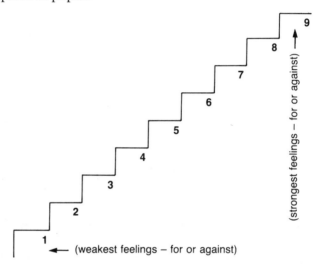

The lowest step is meant to symbolise the weakest emotional reaction – either positive or negative – the highest step the strongest one.

Step 2: The teacher presents a series of statements (see below) which call for value judgements by the students. Each statement is characterised by a key word. After hearing each statement the students enter the key word on their values ladder according to the strength of their reaction. The teacher does not read the next item until everybody has entered the key word on their ladder. Students may change the position of their key words when new items have been read or rearrange all nine key words at the end.

Step 3: At this stage the students should think about why they decided on such a ranking. They are expected to describe their reactions to individual items.

Statements
- A group of young people engage in shoplifting as a kind of sport. When they are caught they defend their actions by pointing out that shop-owners make high profits anyway. (*shoplifting*)
- A group of students want to do something about nature conservation. They meet regularly and go for walks in the country in order to observe wildlife. (*conservation*)
- A group of women have started to boycott certain products which they believe are heavily contaminated by chemicals, antibiotics and pesticides. They have formed a collective to sell organically grown health food. (*food collective*)
- A doctor regularly cheats on his income tax but gives all the money he saves to a hospital in the African bush. (*income tax*)
- Some poor students use the local buses without paying fares. When they are caught they pay the fines. They say that this is still cheaper than paying for tickets. (*bus fares*)
- An American couple living in Fiji publish a book that shows how the lives of the Fijians have been changed by tourism. They distribute the books to all the schools in Fiji. (*Fiji*)
- Some young people in Britain design colourful car stickers and badges against the destruction of the world by technology and science. (*stickers*)
- A group of lawyers set up an office to provide free legal aid to foreign refugees who want to apply for political asylum. (*legal aid*)
- A newspaper reporter finds out that a manufacturer of fruit juice is mixing dangerous chemicals in his product. His report on the factory is suppressed by his paper when the manufacturer threatens to withdraw his advertisements. (*fruit juice*)

Variations 1: Instead of statements, cartoons, photographs or pictures can be used.

2: All the items – their number may be reduced or increased – can be given to the students on a handout. They can then write each key word on a small slip of paper and move the slips about on the ladder in order to rank them.

3: In a less formal classroom context the ladder can be drawn on the floor with chalk and students asked to stand on the step that corresponds with their strength of reaction. Thus the distribution of different reactions is made visible and can trigger off discussion at each stage.

4: The topical slant of the items can be varied according to the interests of the class, the educational aims of the teacher, etc.

53 Looking for a job

Aims	*Skills* – reading comprehension, speaking
	Language – arguing, reacting to other people's statements (agreeing, disagreeing, contradicting, criticising, doubting, defending one's position, giving in)
	Other – cooperation, role taking
Level	Intermediate/advanced
Organisation	Group work (three to five members) as preparation for 'fishbowl' discussion
Preparation	Handout (see Part 2) for each group
Time	20–40 minutes
Procedure	*Step 1:* The handout is distributed to the groups and the task explained. Each group imagines that they are members of the local council who have to select somebody for the vacant post of social worker at Fairview Estate from the four applications that have been submitted. As a first step the groups decide on their criteria for selection, based on the advertisement and the background information on the handout as well as their own judgement. They then discuss the four applicants and rank them according to their suitability. (10–15 minutes)
	Step 2: Each group selects a speaker who has to explain and defend the choice of his group. All the group speakers meet in the middle to discuss the applicants. If one of the other members of the group feels that he has some better way of arguing the group's position he may replace the speaker of his group. Unless a consensus has been reached amongst the speakers after a given time (15 minutes) a vote is taken by all the participants.
Variations	The activity could be continued with a role play. See No. 117 *Interview for a job*.

54 Personalities (1)

Aims	*Skills* – speaking
	Language – giving reasons, making comparisons
	Other – imagination, general knowledge

Level	Beginners
Organisation	Individuals
Preparation	None
Time	10–15 minutes
Procedure	*Step 1:* The teacher writes the following list of (20–30) names on the board or the overhead projector. She asks the students to select the six personalities they would like to invite to their classroom to give a talk and rank them in order of preference. They write their choices in order on a piece of paper. All the papers are collected.

Mahatma Gandhi	Miss Piggy
Mao Tse Tung	Elvis Presley
William Shakespeare	Liv Ullmann
Queen Elizabeth I	Johann Sebastian Bach
Karl Marx	David Copperfield
Alfred Hitchcock	Frank Sinatra
Margaret Thatcher	Naomi James
Mohammed Ali	Charles Dickens
Buffalo Bill	Walt Disney
John Travolta	Winston Churchill
Ronald Reagan	Fidel Castro
Erica Jong	

	Step 2: When the final list for the whole class has been compiled, students who selected the most popular personalities are asked to explain their choice.
Variations	The activity could be continued with the students writing out interview questions they would like to ask the person of their choice.
Remarks	As the list of names to be given to the students is obviously very dependent on the cultural background and the age group of the students concerned, the names mentioned here can only be tentative suggestions. The teacher will be far more successful in devising a list which is geared towards her students' knowledge and interests.

55 Guarantees

Aims	*Skills* – speaking *Language* – persuading others, praising, giving and asking for reasons, if-clauses *Other* – thinking about one's goal in life, looking ahead

Level	Intermediate/advanced
Organisation	Two teams of equal size (max. 40 students)
Preparation	List of 20 guarantees (see below)
Time	30–40 minutes
Procedure	*Step 1:* The whole class is divided into two teams of equal size. One team consists of brokers, the other team being the clients. Instead of insurance, the brokers try to sell guarantees which assure the buyer that he will reach certain personal goals in his life. The brokers are given a list of guarantees and prices. Each of them should receive one guarantee to handle personally. (In smaller groups each broker has to handle more than one guarantee unless their number is reduced.) The brokers now prepare a short talk – about a minute per speaker – praising the advantages of the particular guarantee they want to sell. The clients are asked to think about the goals they would like to achieve in life and how important the guarantees are.

Health Guarantee £60

Popularity Guarantee £30

Intelligence Guarantee £40

Beauty Guarantee £40

Marriage Guarantee £30

Wealth Guarantee £60

Longevity Guarantee £60

Accident-Free-Life Guarantee £50

Satisfaction Guarantee £50

Stardom Guarantee £60

Friendship Guarantee £60

Self-Fulfilment Guarantee £50

Fun Guarantee £40

Adventure Guarantee £30

Career Guarantee £50

Love Guarantee £60

Sexual Fulfilment Guarantee £50

Patience Guarantee £30

Happy Family Guarantee £40

Joy-of-Living Guarantee £30

Step 2: Brokers and clients sit facing each other. Each client can spend £100 on guarantees. In turn the brokers tell the client about the guarantee they can offer, its advantages and price. The clients make notes.

Step 3: Each client now works out which guarantees he would like to spend his £100 on. He then walks over to the relevant brokers to make his purchases. Each broker has to keep a record of the number of guarantees sold.

Step 4: The results of the sale are written up on the board or the overhead projector in order of popularity. The students who acted as clients are asked to explain their choices and motives.

Variations	*1:* The exercise is repeated (with the same or different

guarantees) by letting the former clients act as brokers and vice versa.

2: Students decide on guarantees and their prices in a brainstorming session before the activity.

3: Instead of personal goals students could be asked to buy guarantees for personal possessions or the lives of people they care for.

56 Good teacher

Aims	*Skills* – speaking *Language* – giving reasons, narrating, describing *Other* – thinking about one's own school life and educational values
Level	Intermediate/advanced
Organisation	Individuals
Preparation	Handout (see Part 2)
Time	15–20 minutes
Procedure	*Step 1:* Each student receives the handout listing ten qualities of a good teacher. He is asked to rank them in order of importance. *Step 2:* Meanwhile the teacher draws the following table on the board:

Quality	1	2	3	4	5	6	7	8	9	10
Discipline	||	||||	|||||	|||	||	|		||	|	

Step 3: Each student calls out his ranking of the qualities, which is marked on the table (e.g. as shown, of the 20 students who participated, two felt that this quality was the most important, four the second, etc.) The end result shows the spread of opinion and clusters of similar rankings.

Step 4: Each quality is now discussed in turn and students who give it a high or very low ranking are called upon to explain why. It is hoped that many students will be able to give examples in order to back up their statements.

Variations For further ideas see No. 47 *Qualities.*

Remarks This is a very valuable activity for students who are training to be teachers as it stimulates discussion about role expectations and self-image connected with the profession.

57 Job prestige

Aims *Skills* – speaking

Language – asking for and giving reasons, agreeing and disagreeing

Other – awareness of the reasons for social prestige

Level Intermediate/advanced

Organisation Pairs

Preparation None

Time 15–20 minutes

Procedure *Step 1:* The teacher outlines the task. 'You are going to be given a list of 14 occupations. You have to rank them according to two criteria. First arrange them in the order in which these jobs are regarded and paid for in our society. Secondly make a list in which you show how important *you* think each job should be.'

dentist	university professor
taxi driver	actor
secretary	nurse
schoolteacher	shop-assistant
policeman	librarian
lawyer	engineer
journalist	farmer

'Work with your neighbour. You should – as far as it is possible – reach agreement in both rankings. Where you cannot agree, mark the difference of opinion on your list.'

Step 2: The results are presented by the students and noted on the board. The first list will probably be very similar in each case, with clusters of high prestige and low prestige job emerging clearly. The ranking of the jobs according to the importance allotted to them by individual students may differ wildly and should stimulate a discussion on the criteria for 'upgrading' or 'downgrading' certain occupations.

Variations   The selection of jobs may be altered in view of the occupational background of the students concerned.

3.2 Discussion games

Activity	Topic type	Level	Organis- ation	Prep- aration	Time in minutes
58 What is being advertised?	fact.	int.	pairs	yes	15–20
59 Mad discussion	fact.	int.	teams	yes	20–30
60 Secret topic	fact.	adv.	pairs/class	no	10–20
61 Word wizard	fact.	int.	indiv./pairs	no	10–15
62 Uses and abuses	fact.	int.	teams	no	10–15
63 Shrinking story	fact.	int.	class	Part 2	20–30
64 Which job?	pers.	int.	groups	no	15–20
65 Futures	pers.*	int.	indiv./groups	Part 2	20–30
66 Comments	pers.*	int.	class	no	15–20
67 Magic shop	pers./fact.	int./adv.	indiv.	yes	15–20
68 Pink versus brown	pers./fact	int.	groups/pairs	no	15–25
69 Tell us a story	pers.*	int.	groups/class	no	20–30
70 What evidence?	pers./fact.	int.	teams/groups	Part 2	20–30
71 Optimists and pessimists	fact.	int.	teams	no	5–15
72 People	fact./pers.	int.	groups	yes	15–25
73 Awards	fact./pers.	int.	class/groups	no	25–45
74 Discussion wheel	fact./pers.	int.	groups	Part 2	15–25
75 Four corners	fact.	int.	class/groups	yes	20–30

pers. = personal; pers.* = more intimate; fact. = factual; int. = intermediate; adv. = advanced; indiv. = individuals; groups = small groups; pairs = two people working together; teams = two large groups of equal size; class = everybody working together; Part 2 = material for the exercise is to be found in Part 2.

Not all of the 18 activities in this section are games in a narrow sense of the word; in some cases they are game-like discussions or game-like exercises that lead to discussions. Quite often the same exercise can be used for discussion of serious questions as well as for playing with ideas and language. The main intention of all these exercises is, of course, to get the students to talk and to stimulate their interest and imagination. Thus some discussion games make the students think about their values and priorities (e.g. No. 65 *Futures* and No. 67 *Magic shop*), others help them learn something about themselves (e.g. No. 64 *Which job?* and No. 69 *Tell us a story*) and play with words (e.g. No. 61 *Word wizard*). Nearly all of them demand a certain degree of flexibility in the foreign language and are structured in such a way that everyone will get a turn.

To get everybody involved in the discussion may

occasionally be difficult. You could ask the students to hand round an object (e.g. a knotted scarf or a paper weight) and agree on the rule that whoever is holding the object has to contribute something to the discussion. It is not to be expected that each student will be able to think of something new to say, but in order to be able to say things like 'I agree with . . .' or 'I don't agree with . . . because', he has to listen carefully throughout the discussion. Other ways of organising discussions are mentioned in the general introduction (see pp. 9–10).

As regards their language learning aims, the discussion games in this section differ quite substantially from one another. However, a common feature is that students have to give reasons for their views. Some discussion games can only be played by advanced learners who have a good command of the foreign language (e.g. No. 60 *Secret topic*).

You can also use discussion games to improve the atmosphere in your class and help students cooperate better with each other. Sometimes certain people subconsciously adopt particular roles in discussion. If you feel that is the case, ask a few students to observe some of the others during the next discussion and to note down who takes which role. Possible roles are:

– initiator (starts the discussion, makes suggestions and tries to move the discussion along by asking questions)
– summariser (sums up in between; explains the points where there is agreement or disagreement in the group)
– grumbler (criticises both content and procedure of the discussion)
– rambler (rambles on about trivial side-issues; can hardly be stopped)
– silent member (does not talk at all except possibly to his neighbour; sometimes these people show quite clearly by their facial expressions what they think about the contributions of others)
– clown (makes fun of everything; tells jokes)
– mediator (tries to find compromises between different factions; stresses the common ground)
– hesitator (cannot find a clear view of his own; hesitates when talking)

You can probably think of more types yourself. When the observers have noted some of the typical roles present in discussions in your class the next step is to make the students realise that they are adopting certain roles. This can be done either by making use of a tape or a video tape recording of the next discussion or by keeping detailed minutes. Then a role play can be acted out where each participant in the discussion has to play a role which the others do not know about. After the role play these roles are guessed.

Many of the discussion games may lead to oral or written follow-up activities: after doing No. 65 *Futures*, an essay on one's hopes or fears for the future could be set; in connection with No. 58 *What is being advertised?*, the students could make up their own advertisements; No. 73 *Awards* could be followed by a panel discussion.

Quite a number of the problem-solving activities, ranking exercises and values clarification techniques serve as stimuli for discussion as long as they generate controversial opinions amongst the students. For example, activity No. 38 *Getting it together* presents the participants with an experience (i.e. an attempt at working without communication) which is worth discussing afterwards. Further suggestions are to be found in *Learning for Change* 1977 and Stanford and Stanford 1969.

58 What is being advertised?

Aims	*Skills* – speaking, writing *Language* – making conjectures, expressing probability, giving reasons *Other* – making notes, discovering some advertising techniques
Level	Intermediate
Organisation	Pairs
Preparation	A number of different advertisements (cut out from magazines) from which all names and pictures of the products advertised have been removed, half as many advertisements as there are students. (Don't throw away the bits that have been cut out.)
Time	15–20 minutes
Procedure	*Step 1:* Each pair of students receives one advertisement. The partners discuss what product the advertisement could be for and why they think so. One of each pair makes some notes. After about five minutes the advertisements are exchanged

and each pair of students discusses another advertisement in the same way.

Step 2: Taking turns, each pair of students show their second advertisement to the rest of the class and report their ideas on the product being advertised. The two students who discussed this particular advertisement in the first round say where they agree or disagree and give reasons. When all the advertisements have been discussed the teacher gives the solutions (by presenting the cut-out parts of each advertisement).

Remarks   When the students are making suggestions about the type of product being advertised by, for example, idyllic scenes in the country, their attention can be drawn to the associations which certain pictures give us (e.g. waterfall – clean air, health – cigarettes).

59   Mad discussion

Aims   *Skills* – speaking
Language – giving reasons, describing advantages and disadvantages, contradicting
Other – imagination, fun

Level   Intermediate

Organisation   Teams

Preparation   Pieces of paper with one word written on them (see below)

Time   20–30 minutes

Procedure   *Step 1:* The class is divided into teams. One student from each team comes forward. Each chooses a piece of paper with a topic on it. He then has three minutes to argue with the student from the other team about which is more important for mankind, e.g. alsatians or pizzas. Possible topics: flowers, New York, operas, ships, plastic spoons, birthday cards, passports, watches, modern art, detective novels, schools, bakers, socks, zips, paper, the wheel, etc.

Step 2: (optional) A jury decides who has put the best arguments and awards points for each team. Then the next two students continue with new topics.

Remarks   In this game it is important not only to put forward good arguments for one's own case but to try and contradict the opponent's point of view.

60 Secret topic

Aims	*Skills* – speaking
	Language – all elements
	Other – talking without coming to the point, fun, imagination
Level	Advanced
Organisation	Pairs, class
Preparation	None
Time	10–20 minutes
Procedure	*Step 1:* Two students agree on a topic they want to talk about without telling the others what it is.
	Step 2: The two students start discussing their topic without mentioning it. The others listen. Anyone in the rest of the group who thinks he knows what they are talking about, joins in their conversation. When about a third or half of the class have joined in, the game is stopped.
Variations	*1:* Students who think they know the secret topic have to write it on a piece of paper and show it to the two students before they are accepted.
	2: The game can be played in teams and points awarded according to the number of people who find out the secret topic.

61 Word wizard

Aims	*Skills* – speaking, writing
	Language – individual words
	Other – imagination, feeling for words, communicating with very few words
Level	Intermediate
Organisation	Individuals, pairs
Preparation	None
Time	10–15 minutes
Procedure	*Step 1:* The teacher asks the class to imagine the following situation: 'A wizard has taken away all the words from the world. Everybody can keep just four words. Choose four words which you would like to keep and write them down.'
	Step 2: Each student finds a partner and tries to communicate using only his four words. The pairs share their words with each other so that now both have eight words they can use. Each student shares his eight words with

another student, so that both have 16, then twice more. In the end everybody has 64 words.

    Step 3: Either alone or with a partner the students write a story or poem using only their words. These stories/poems are read out or stuck up on the wall.

Remarks   (Idea adapted from Brandes and Phillips 1979.)

62 Uses and abuses

Aims   *Skills* – speaking
    Language – declarative sentences, -ing form
    Other – imagination

Level   Intermediate

Organisation   Teams

Preparation   None

Time   10–15 minutes

Procedure   *Step 1:* The teacher and the class prepare two lists (of about 20 items), which are written up by secretaries from the two teams. List A contains people and animals, list B, objects.

Example:

A	B
teacher	book
mother	walking stick
shop-assistant	plaster
baby	50p coin
elephant	pen
crocodile	loaf of bread
soldier	car
dustman	cactus
farmer	apple pie
old woman	glass of beer
nurse	safety pin

    Step 2: The two teams sit facing each other. The secretary from team 1 starts by inserting one word from list A and one from list B into one of the two sentence patterns:

What can a/an A do with a/an B?

Why does a/an A need a/an B?

The students in team 2 must find three answers quickly. Then their secretary makes up a new question for team 1. The

secretary crosses out the words that have been used. The
game is finished when all the words have been used up.

Variations   *1:* The sentence patterns can be extended by adding a place,
e.g.
Why does a/an A need a/an B in C?
  2: A system of scoring can be introduced.
  3: Students can pass each other a knotted scarf and play
the game according to the rules of volleyball or another sport.
(In volleyball, each of the two teams may only touch the ball
three times before it *has to* be played to the opposite team.)
Each team can have up to three answers before throwing the
'ball' to the other team.

Remarks   Having a fixed sentence pattern may sometimes result in
slightly odd sentences.

63 Shrinking story

Aims   *Skills* – speaking, listening comprehension
Language – all elements
Other – memory, insight into the process of communication

Level   Intermediate

Organisation   Class

Preparation   Story (see Part 2) or picture

Time   20–30 minutes

Procedure   *Step 1:* Five students are asked to leave the room. The rest of
the class is read the story (or played a recording). They listen
to the story twice and after the second reading agree on a few
important points which a summary of the story should
contain. These are written down by everyone.

  Step 2: The first student is asked to come in and listens to
the story (once). The second student is called in and hears the
story from the first student while the class notes down which
of the important points have been mentioned. Student 2 then
tells the story to student 3, student 3 to student 4, and student
4 to the last one. Student 5 tells the story to the class.

  Step 3: Using their notes, the students who were listening
and observing report on the changes in the story. Then the
original is read (played) once again.

Variations   *1:* Instead of telling a story, a picture could be described and
drawn by the last student.
  2: If a cassette recorder is available all the versions of the
story can be recorded and compared.

79

64 Which job?

Aims   *Skills* – speaking
Language – conditional, discussing, giving reasons, names of jobs
Other – getting to know each other, learning something about oneself

Level   Intermediate

Organisation   Groups of six students

Preparation   None

Time   15–20 minutes

Procedure   *Step 1:* The students work together in groups. Each group member writes down the ideal job for himself and for everybody else in the group.

    Step 2: The job lists are read out and discussed in the groups. Students explain why they feel the 'ideal jobs' suggested for them would/would not be ideal.

65 Futures

Aims   *Skills* – writing, speaking
Language – future tense, making comparisons
Other – thinking about the world around us and how we are affected by what happens there

Level   Intermediate

Organisation   Individuals, groups

Preparation   Two charts for each student (see Part 2)

Time   20–30 minutes

Procedure   *Step 1:* Each student receives two copies of the chart. He is asked to fill in one with *Good Things*, the other with *Bad Things* by writing examples in each square.

    Step 2: When students have finished, they form groups to share and discuss their hopes and fears for the future. Each group can focus on one time period and report the good and bad feelings of their group.

Variations   Instead of writing, the students can draw sketches.

Remarks   It is important to see the connections between the various squares. What happens in the world now may well affect our children in twenty years' time.
(Idea adapted from *Learning for Change* 1977.)

66 Comments

Aims	*Skills* – writing, speaking
	Language – all elements, expressing emotions
	Other – getting to know each other
Level	Intermediate
Organisation	Class
Preparation	None
Time	15–20 minutes
Procedure	*Step 1:* Every student writes his name at the top of a piece of paper. All the papers are collected, shuffled and redistributed.
	Step 2: Now every student writes a comment (a compliment, a question, a statement) under the name of the person. The papers are again collected and redistributed, so that everyone can write a second comment. The teacher (or a student) now collects all the papers.
	Step 3: The papers are read out one after the other and a discussion follows. How did the people concerned feel? Were the comments fair/superficial/critical/supportive?
Variations	Instead of having the discussion after all the comments have been read out, a short conversation can follow each comment.
Remarks	For this exercise there should be a supportive atmosphere within the class.

67 Magic shop

Aims	*Skills* – speaking
	Language – if-clauses, arguing, praising something
	Other – learning something about one's own values
Level	Intermediate/advanced
Organisation	Individuals
Preparation	Slips of paper with positive human qualities written on them (see below), three times as many slips as there are students (qualities may occur more than once)
Time	15–20 minutes
Procedure	*Step 1:* Each student receives three slips of paper, each with a positive human quality on it, e.g. honesty, intelligence, fairness, humour, health, beauty, stubbornness, curiosity, cheerfulness, gentleness, humility, optimism, perseverance, politeness, hospitality, helpfulness, thoughtfulness, wisdom, justice, friendliness, adaptability, charity.

Step 2: Each student decides which of his three qualities he would like to keep and which to exchange for others. Students then barter with different people.

Step 3: After 10 minutes of bartering, students report on which qualities they received, which ones they kept and whether they are happy with their present one(s) (they may have more or fewer than three).

68 Pink versus brown

Aims	*Skills* – speaking
	Language – contradicting, praising something, giving reasons
	Other – fun, imagination
Level	Intermediate
Organisation	Groups, pairs
Preparation	None
Time	15–25 minutes
Procedure	*Step 1:* Students whose favourite colours are the same should work together. They describe to each other why they like this particular colour better than any other.
	Step 2: Students leave their groups and pair up with someone from a different group. Each partner argues for his favourite colour and tries to convince the other one of its qualities.
Variations	Step 1 can be left out.

69 Tell us a story

Aims	*Skills* – speaking
	Language – descriptive sentences
	Other – fun
Level	Intermediate
Organisation	Groups of four to seven students, class
Preparation	None
Time	20–30 minutes
Procedure	*Step 1:* The students work together in groups. Each member of the group is asked to tell his version of a story with the same basic plot. Each student makes notes on what his right-hand neighbour says. The basic stages of the story are as follows:

You are walking in a wood; describe what it is like. Then you come to some water; describe what it is like. What do you feel about this water and what do you do about it? Next you find a key. Describe it and say what you would do with it. At the end of the wood there is a barrier. What is it like? What is on the other side? What do you do about it?

Step 2: When everyone has told his story the teacher reveals how each episode of the story might be interpreted:

The wood gives an indication of the storyteller's view of life. Is it described as dark and frightening or sunlit and happy? Full of menace, or full of hopeful possibilities? It depends on attitudes to living.

The water is sex. Is it dark and dirty or lovely and sparkling? Deep or shallow? Frightening, but pleasantly so? Do you dive right in or keep well out?

The key is worldly success and ambition to attain it. Do you see a big golden key or a dreary little Yale key? Is it rusty or shining? Do you reject or hold on to it? Do you use it immediately in some way, or later on, perhaps finding a box full of treasure to go with it, or do you just hopefully tuck it in your pocket? Do you give it away to someone you think may want it?

The barrier is death, the view beyond a picture of the life hereafter. (When I first played this game, I 'saw' a range of formidable mountains, and nothing beyond. I disliked it intensely, and turned round and went back the way I'd come. There's hope!)

Remarks This activity should not be taken too seriously. It is not meant to provide a psychoanalyst's couch for the foreign language classroom!

70 What evidence?

Aims	*Skills* – speaking
	Language – discussing, giving reasons, agreeing and disagreeing
	Other – thinking about questions of credibility, evaluating information
Level	Intermediate
Organisation	Teams or groups
Preparation	A handout for each group (see Part 2)
Time	20–30 minutes

Procedure   *Step 1:* Each team or group receives a copy of the handout. The students now have to discuss what evidence each of them would accept as regards the truth of each statement. They should not discuss whether they believe that a statement is true but what evidence would convince them. If the students cannot agree on acceptable proof they should note down their differences of opinion.

Step 2: When all the statements have been discussed, the groups report back to the whole class.

Remarks   (Idea adapted from Krupar 1973.)

71   Optimists and pessimists

Aims   *Skills* – speaking
Language – expressing different points of view
Other – imagination, fun

Level   Intermediate

Organisation   Two teams

Preparation   None

Time   5–15 minutes

Procedure   *Step 1:* One student from team 1 (optimists) begins by giving a statement, e.g. 'It is good for your health if you do some sport.' Then one student from the other team (pessimists) gives the other point of view, e.g. 'But sports like boxing or car racing are dangerous.' The pessimists continue with a new – pessimistic – statement, which the optimists have to react to.

Step 2: After a few minutes of exchanging statements, the students are asked if they found it difficult to adopt one point of view throughout. They could also mention those statements which went against their personal viewpoint.

Variations   A good follow-up activity is I/You/He statements like:
I don't dance very well.
You haven't got much feeling for rhythm.
He tramples on his partner's feet.
Or:
I enjoy eating.
You are a bit overweight.
He is fat.

72 People

Aims	*Skills* – writing
	Language – past tense, present tense, describing someone
	Other – imagination
Level	Intermediate
Organisation	Groups of three to four students
Preparation	Photos of different people (cut out from magazines or your own snapshots), one photo per group
Time	15–25 minutes
Procedure	*Step 1:* Each group receives a photo and is asked to write a curriculum vitae for the person in the picture. The students should mainly imagine the person's present interests and lifestyle. When they have finished with the first picture, photos are exchanged between groups. Each group works with three pictures.
	Step 2: The results of the group work are read out and discussed. Which lives were seen in a similar way by the three groups? Which pictures were interpreted differently?
Remarks	If the teacher uses photographs of people she knows, she could tell the students how far off the mark they are.

73 Awards

Aims	*Skills* – speaking
	Language – describing someone, reporting someone's activities, giving reasons, contradicting, stating preferences, agreeing and disagreeing
	Other – thinking of praiseworthy qualities in ordinary people
Level	Intermediate
Organisation	Class, groups of four to six students
Preparation	None
Time	25–45 minutes
Procedure	*Step 1:* The students talk about the awards they can think of (awards for looks, such as 'Miss World, for bravery, etc.).
	Step 2: Using brainstorming techniques (see No. 87 *Brainstorming*) the class try to think of many more possible awards (e.g. Smile Award, Help Award, Listening Award). All awards (they should be for positive qualities) are listed on the blackboard.
	Step 3: Groups are formed and each group decides on two categories of award they would like to find candidates for.

Step 4: Now each group member describes one candidate for each award. (These should be people he knows personally.) Another group member takes down some notes. When everybody has finished, the qualities of all the people suggested for awards are discussed. The group members have to agree on who to give the awards to.

Step 5: Each group reports its results to the class. A short discussion of the reasons for choosing these people follows.

74 Discussion wheel

Aims	*Skills* – speaking
	Language – discussing
	Other – (dependent on the topics)
Level	Intermediate
Organisation	Groups of six students
Preparation	One handout for each group (see Part 2), three dice per group
Time	15–25 minutes
Procedure	Each group receives a copy of the handout and three dice. Each group member is given a number from 1 to 6. The dice are thrown; two dice indicate the students who start the discussion, the third die indicates the topic they have to talk about. After a short while the other group members can join the discussion. Every topic on the wheel should be discussed at least once. If the topic die shows the number 5, the two students choose their own discussion topic.
Variations	*1:* Instead of writing the discussion topics on the discussion wheel, they can be put on small cards and laid face down on the wheel.
	2: More factual or more personal topics can be chosen.

75 Four corners

Aims	*Skills* – speaking
	Language – giving reasons, agreeing and disagreeing
	Other – getting to know each other
Level	Intermediate
Organisation	Class, groups
Preparation	Masking tape, 20 big pieces of paper with one word on each

(see below). The classroom should be cleared of tables and chairs.

Time 20–30 minutes

Procedure *Step 1:* The teacher fixes a piece of paper to the wall in each of the four corners of the room. The words on each piece of paper should belong to the same category, e.g. colours: WHITE, RED, BROWN, PURPLE; or writers: GEORGE ORWELL, ARTHUR HAILEY, WILLIAM WORDSWORTH, LEONARD COHEN. Other possible categories for the signs are: types of music, articles of clothing, tools, cities, countries, drinks, numbers, animals, etc.

Step 2: The students are asked to read all four signs and stand in the corner which suits them best. All the students in one corner interview each other about why they chose this one. When the next four signs are hung up everyone chooses again.

Step 3: At the end a short discussion can follow on which students often chose the same corner, which students never met, etc.

Variations Instead of single words, statements, quotations, proverbs or drawings can be used.

3.3 Values clarification techniques

Activity	Topic type	Level	Organis- ation	Prep- aration	Time in minutes
76 Personalities (2)	pers.*	int.	indiv./class	no	10–30
77 Lifestyle	pers.*	beg./int.	pairs	yes	10–15
78 Aims in life	pers.*	int.	indiv./groups	Part 2	15–20
79 Twenty things I'd like to do	pers.	int.	indiv.	no	20–30
80 Values continuum	pers.	int.	indiv./class	Part 2	15–20
81 Spending money	pers.	int.	indiv./groups	no	10–25
82 Miracle workers	pers.*	int.	indiv./groups/ class	Part 2	20–40
83 Unfinished sentences	pers.	int.	pairs	Part 2	10–20
84 I'd rather be . . .	pers.*	int.	class	yes	5–15
85 Ideal day	pers.	int.	indiv.	no	20–30
86 Values topics	pers.	int.	groups	Part 2	30

pers. = personal; pers.* = more intimate; beg. = beginners; int. = intermediate; indiv. = individuals; groups = small groups; pairs = two people working together; class = everybody working together; Part 2 = material for the exercise is to be found in Part 2.

The activities in this section are based on the principle of the 'values clarification approach' which originated in the USA (see Howe and Howe 1975, Simon et al 1972). It is one of the assumptions of this approach that school must help young people to become aware of their own values and to act according to them. The psychologist Louis Raths distinguishes between three main stages in this process: 'Prizing one's beliefs and behaviours, . . . choosing one's beliefs and behaviours, . . . acting on one's beliefs' (Simon et al 1972, p. 19). Personal values relate both to one's own personality and to the outside world, including such areas as school, leisure activities or politics. Adults as well as young people may not always be consciously aware of their beliefs and so learners of all ages may find that the activities in this section help them to discover something about themselves.

The eleven activities in this section mainly concern the prizing and choosing of values; acting on one's beliefs cannot be learnt so easily in the foreign language class. The individual tasks appeal directly to the learners, who have to be prepared to talk about their feelings and attitudes. On the one hand this may be a very motivating experience, because the students feel that they are communicating about something meaningful, as well as being taken seriously as people; on the other hand a situation in which the participants have to reveal some of their more 'private' thoughts may appear threatening. Thus it is essential to do these exercises in a supportive and relaxed atmosphere. You may help create this atmosphere by joining in some of the exercises and sharing your values with your students. You should also remind your students of the guideline (see Introduction, p. 7) that nobody has to answer embarrassing questions, and that the right to refuse to answer is granted to everyone in these exercises. The educational bias of values clarification techniques makes it easier to integrate them into a democratic style of teaching than more traditional teacher-centred methods.

As regards the language items practised in these exercises, speech acts like expressing likes and dislikes, stating one's opinions and giving/asking for reasons occur throughout. Skills like note taking are also practised, because students are often asked to jot down their ideas and feelings.

Values clarification techniques share some characteristics with ranking exercises, but the latter are more structured and predictable. Further suggestions for values clarification techniques can be found in Green 1975, Howe and Howe 1975, *Learning for Change* 1977, Moskowitz 1978, Papalia 1976b, Simon et al 1972.

76 Personalities (2)

Aims	*Skills* – speaking, writing
	Language – descriptive sentences, past tense (reported speech)
	Other – acknowledging the influence other people have on us, note taking
Level	Intermediate
Organisation	Individuals, class
Preparation	None
Time	10–30 minutes
Procedure	*Step 1:* The students are asked to think about their lives and the people they know/have known. Each student should find at least two people who have influenced him in his life. These may be his parents, other relations, friends, or personalities from history or literature. He should note down some points in order to be able to tell the rest of the class briefly how these people have influenced him.

Step 2: Each student in turn says a few sentences about these
people. A discussion and/or question may follow each speaker.
Remarks Emphasis should be given to positive influences.

77 Lifestyle

Aims *Skills* – speaking
Language – giving reasons, stating likes and dislikes
Other – thinking about one's priorities
Level Beginners/intermediate
Organisation Pairs
Preparation Students are asked a day or so beforehand to bring along
three objects which are important or significant for them.
Time 10–15 minutes
Procedure *Step 1:* Students work with a partner. Each of them explains
the use/purpose of the three objects he has brought with him
and says why they are important and significant for him.
Both partners then talk about similarities and differences
between their choice of objects.
Step 2: A few of the students present their partner's objects
and explain their significance to the rest of the group.
Variations *1:* Instead of real objects, drawings or photographs (cut out
of magazines or catalogues) may be used.
2: Before the paired discussion starts, a kind of speculating
or guessing game can be conducted, where the three objects
of a student whose identity is not revealed are shown, and
suggestions about their significance are made.

78 Aims in life

Aims *Skills* – writing, speaking
Language – asking for and giving reasons, expressing
intentions and desires
Other – making notes, thinking about one's aims in life
Level Intermediate
Organisation Individuals, groups
Preparation A handout for each student (see Part 2)
Time 15–20 minutes
Procedure *Step 1:* Each student fills in the blanks in the handout by first
choosing the area of his aims, i.e. travel, job or family, etc.,

and then by making a few notes on what he wants to achieve within this area in the time specified.

Step 2: When everybody has filled in the handout with at least one aim for each of the three time periods given, small groups are formed. The students discuss and defend their aims in the groups.

Variations Instead of group discussion, a class discussion can follow Step 1. Possible points to be raised: Are personal aims more important than general ones? Which kind of aims can we do most about ourselves? In which areas does chance play a part?

79 Twenty things I'd like to do

Aims *Skills* – writing, speaking
Language – expressing likes and dislikes
Other – analysing one's likes

Level Intermediate

Organisation Individuals

Preparation None

Time 20–30 minutes

Procedure *Step 1:* The students are asked to write a list of 20 things they would like to do. These can be ordinary activities like eating a lot of icecream or more exotic dreams like going for a trip in a balloon. They should jot down anything that comes to mind, writing the activities one under the other. These lists will remain private.

Step 2: The students are asked to code their lists by putting one or more of the following symbols in front of them:

£   if the activity is expensive

WF   if the activity involves other people (WF = with friends)

A   if they would do this on their own (A = alone)

M or F   if they think their mother (M) or father (F) would enjoy this, too

X   if the activity is at all physically or mentally harmful (e.g. smoking)

Step 3: Now the students should think about the distribution of these symbols on their lists and continue the following stem sentences:

I have learnt from this exercise   I am pleased that . . .
    that . . .   I am worried that . . .
I am surprised that . . .   I don't mind that . . .

91

The completed sentences are collected by the teacher and
individual ones read out, provided they contain a stimulus for
discussion.

Variations *1:* Students may want to make suggestions for other ways of
coding.

2: The lists are made up of things the students would *not*
like to do.

80 Values continuum

Aims *Skills* – reading comprehension, speaking
Language – giving reasons, expressing agreement and
disagreement
Other – classifying one's values
Level Intermediate
Organisation Individuals, class
Preparation A handout for each student (see Part 2)
Time 15–20 minutes
Procedure *Step 1:* Each student fills in the handout by marking on his
agreement or disagreement with each statement.

Step 2: The distribution of agreements and disagreements
within the class is revealed and differences of opinion are
discussed.

Step 3: (optional) Students are asked to look at their
handouts again and note those statements where they agreed
or disagreed very strongly. They can use unfinished sentences
as in No. 79 *Twenty things I'd like to do* to sum up their
insights.
Variations Instead of statements (which can of course be adapted to any
course work being done at the time) proverbs or sayings can
be used.

81 Spending money

Aims *Skills* – speaking
Language – asking for and giving reasons
Other – thinking about one's priorities
Level Intermediate
Organisation Individuals, groups
Preparation None
Time 10–25 minutes

Procedure *Step 1:* Each student writes down what he would spend a given sum of money on, e.g. 50p, £2, £5, £20, £50, £100, £500, £1,000, £5,000, £100,000.
  Step 2: Students sit together in small groups and describe what they have decided to buy with a particular amount of money and why they would like to make this purchase.

Variations Students are given a choice of five to eight items for each sum, e.g. for £2 you could buy (a) a cinema ticket for the latest James Bond film, (b) a paperback novel, (c) a pack of cards, (d) a T-shirt, (e) an LP with a selection of pop songs, (f) a Chinese meal, (g) a pot plant. These items can be adapted to suit the group of students.

82 Miracle workers

Aims *Skills* – reading comprehension, speaking
  Language – giving and asking for reasons, agreeing and disagreeing
  Other – thinking about aims and priorities in one's life

Level Intermediate

Organisation Individuals, small groups or class

Preparation A handout for each student (see Part 2)

Time 20–40 minutes

Procedure *Step 1:* Each student receives a handout with the names and description of 15 miracle workers. Each student should divide them into three groups of five:
  (a) the five most desirable ones for himself, whose services he would like to obtain;
  (b) the next most interesting ones;
  (c) the five least desirable ones.
  Step 2: In small groups or the whole class together, students compare their lists and try to find out if they agree on a few not very desirable miracle workers. They should try and discover a pattern in their choices, e.g. 'What values are dominant in your choice of the desirable miracle workers?'
  Step 3: Individual students talk about one particular miracle worker and tell the class which category he is in and why they put him there.
  Step 4: (optional) A few students take over the roles of their most valued miracle workers and hold a mock discussion as to who is most important for mankind.

Remarks (Idea adapted from Simon et al 1972.)

83 Unfinished sentences

Aims	*Skills* – speaking, reading comprehension *Language* – expressing emotions and thoughts, agreeing and disagreeing (a great number of structures) *Other* – getting to know oneself and others better
Level	Intermediate
Organisation	Pairs (two teams of equal size arranged in the 'onion' formation, see Introduction, p. 9)
Preparation	A handout for each student (see Part 2)
Time	10–20 minutes
Procedure	The class is divided into two teams of equal size. The chairs are arranged in two circles, one inside the other, facing each other. Each student receives a handout and sits on a chair. There are always two students facing each other. They each continue the first of the unfinished sentences on the handout and talk about their sentences. The students in the outer circle then all move one chair to the left and do the second sentence with a new partner. They continue moving on after each sentence until all the sentences have been discussed.
Variations	If a particular grammatical structure is to be practised, e.g. the infinitive or if-clauses, sentences using this structure may be chosen.

84 I'd rather be . . .

Aims	*Skills* – speaking *Language* – asking for and giving reasons *Other* – fun
Level	Intermediate
Organisation	Class
Preparation	A list of word pairs (nouns, adjectives) for the teacher
Time	5–15 minutes
Procedure	The teacher reads out pairs of 'opposites' from her list and asks the students which ones they would rather be. The students should also give a reason for their choice. Possible word pairs:

soft	– hard	hammer	– nail
glass	– wood	rose	– cactus
water	– fire	mineral water	– whisky
bitter	– sweet	square	– round
beauty	– ugliness	cold	– hot

sparrow — snail	candle — neon light
hawk — mouse	village — city
chicken — egg	lemon — potato

Variations The same activity is possible with verbs, e.g. sell – buy, make – break, arrive – leave, etc.

85 Ideal day

Aims *Skills* – writing, listening comprehension, reading aloud
Language – all elements
Other – day-dreaming, imagination
Level Intermediate
Organisation Individuals
Preparation None
Time 20–30 minutes
Procedure *Step 1:* Students are asked to write a description of an ideal day. They can choose freely the places they would like to be in, their activities and the company they would like to have.
   Step 2: Some students read out their descriptions.
Variations Other topics to write about are: my ideal flat/house, an ideal holiday, an ideal friend.

86 Values topics

Aims *Skills* – speaking
Language – describing something, asking questions
Other – fun, getting to know each other better
Level Intermediate
Organisation Groups of three to five students
Preparation A handout with the board game (see Part 2), a die and counters for each group
Time 30 minutes
Procedure The rules of the game are simple. Each player throws the die and moves his counter forward accordingly. If his counter lands on a white square he tells the others in the group something about the topic on the square. If he lands on a 'free question' square one of the other students may ask him a question. The player concerned is allowed to refuse to answer the question, but he should say why he won't answer it.

3.4 Thinking strategies

Activity	Topic type	Level	Organis- ation	Prep- aration	Time in minutes
87 Brainstorming	fact.	int.	groups	no	5–15
88 PMI	fact.	int.	indiv./pairs/class	no	10–20
89 Consequences	fact.	int.	groups/class	yes	10–20
90 Alternatives	fact.	int.	class	yes	5–20
91 Viewpoints	fact.	int.	groups	Part 2	15–20

fact. = factual; int. = intermediate; indiv. = individuals; groups = small groups; pairs = two people working together; class = everybody working together; Part 2 = material for the exercise is to be found in Part 2.

In the last decade Edward de Bono has repeatedly demanded that thinking should be taught in schools. His main intention is to change our rigid way of thinking and make us learn to think creatively. Some of the activities in this section are taken from his thinking course for schools (de Bono 1973). Brainstorming, although also mentioned by de Bono, is a technique that has been used widely in psychology and cannot be attributed to him.

The thinking strategies included here resemble each other in that different ideas have to be collected by the participants in the first stage. In the second stage these ideas have to be ordered and evaluated. It is obvious that there is ample opportunity to use the foreign language at both stages. Apart from the speech acts of agreeing and disagreeing, suggesting, etc. these exercises practise all forms of comparison and the conditional.

Thinking strategies can be linked with ranking exercises (see section 3.1) and role play. Further suggestions can be found in de Bono 1973.

87 Brainstorming

Aims	*Skills* – speaking, writing
	Language – conditional, making suggestions
	Other – imagination, practice of important thinking skills
Level	Intermediate
Organisation	Groups of four to seven students
Preparation	None
Time	5–15 minutes

Procedure   *Step 1:* The class is divided into groups. Each group receives the same task. Possible tasks are:
(a) How many possible uses can you find for a paper clip (plastic bag/wooden coat hanger/teacup/pencil/sheet of typing paper/matchbox, etc.)?
(b) You have to make an important phone call but you have no change. How many ways can you find of getting the money for the call?
(c) How many ways can you find of opening a wine bottle without a corkscrew?
(d) How many ways can you find of having a cheap holiday?
The groups work on the task for a few minutes, collecting as many ideas as possible without commenting on them or evaluating them. *All* the ideas are written down by the group secretary.
   Step 2: Each group reads out their list of ideas. The ideas are written on the board.
   Step 3: The groups choose five ideas from the complete list (either the most original or the most practical ones) and rank them.

Variations   *1:* After Step 1 the groups exchange their lists of ideas. Each group ranks the ideas on its new list according to a common criterion, e.g. practicability, costs, simplicity, danger, etc.
   2: Each group chooses an idea and discusses it according to the procedure in No. 89 *Consequences.*

Remarks   Brainstorming increases mental flexibility and encourages original thinking. It is a useful strategy for a great number of teaching situations.

88 PMI

Aims   *Skills* – speaking, writing
Language – conditional, comparatives, making suggestions
Other – note taking, thinking creatively
Level   Intermediate
Organisation   Individuals, pairs, class
Preparation   None
Time   10–20 minutes
Procedure   *Step 1:* The students have to think of the plus points (P), minus points (M) and interesting points (I) of an idea. The teacher gives the class an idea and then everybody works on their own for a few minutes. Possible ideas:

A new law is passed that forbids smoking in all public places.
Every family is only allowed to have meat once a week.
People should wear badges to show what mood they are in.
To save energy public buildings like post offices, stations, schools and offices are no longer heated.
A scientist discovers a way of making gold cheaply.
Boys are only allowed to wear green clothes, girls, blue clothes.
Children over 5 are given the vote.
Planes do not work any more. They all crash after take-off.
Step 2: Each student works with a partner and they share their ideas.
Step 3: The ideas are discussed with the whole class.

Variations	*1:* After Step 1, small groups are formed who evaluate the ideas of other students.
	2: Small groups rank the points mentioned by other students.
Remarks	(Idea adapted from de Bono 1973.)

89 Consequences

Aims	*Skills* – speaking
	Language – future tense, conditional
	Other – thinking creatively
Level	Intermediate
Organisation	Groups of three to six students, class
Preparation	As many cards with an action on as there are groups
Time	10–20 minutes
Procedure	*Step 1:* The teacher divides the class into groups. She gives each group an action card. Examples: A 25-hour working week is introduced. A lorry driver empties a tankful of poisonous waste into the river near a town. Animal merchants catch the last animals of a dying species and sell them to zoos in Europe and North America. Men can get maternity leave (paternity leave) like women. Robots that can do housework are built. Scientists discover that cancer is caused by pollution. A group of boys always use the bus or tram without paying. Each group now has to think of all the possible long-term and short-term consequences this action may have. The group secretary writes down all the consequences.

Step 2: When the group cannot think of any more consequences they exchange cards with another group. With each new card a different group member becomes secretary.

Step 3: The consequences of each action are shared and discussed with the whole class.

Variations   Each student can work out consequences on his own before working in a group.

Remarks   It should be stressed that there is rarely a chain of events triggered by one action alone. This technique is slightly misleading as it does not take complex situations and reasons for actions into account. Nevertheless it may help students realise that simple actions have far-reaching consequences. For some classes it can be helpful to give the students a handout to be filled in, like the one that follows. (Idea adapted from de Bono 1973.)

Action			
C O N S E Q U E N C E S	Next few days	Next year	Next 20 years

90 Alternatives

Aims   *Skills* – speaking, writing
Language – conditional, making suggestions
Other – creative thinking, mental flexibility
Level   Intermediate
Organisation   Class (small groups)
Preparation   List of problem situations for the teacher (see examples below)
Time   5–20 minutes
Procedure   *Step 1:* The teacher presents a problem situation to the class and asks the students to think of as many courses of action as possible for the people involved.

Step 2: Individual students present their suggestions and a complete list is compiled (in note form) on the board or overhead projector.

Step 3: (*optional*) Students work together in small groups and rank all the suggestions in order of preference. They then discuss what consequences the five most popular suggestions will have. The rank orders and consequences of individual groups are compared.

Possible problem situations:

(a) You hear from a friend that someone is saying nasty things about you. What can you do?

(b) Some money was stolen in the classroom recently. The thief has not been found. Your teacher treats you differently from before and you think she suspects that you took the money. You did not, but you know who took it. What can you do?

(c) Your friend has bought a new coat. You think it is really ugly and does not suit her. However, you know it was very expensive and your friend is easily offended. What can you say?

(d) You see somebody dumping rubbish in the countryside. What can you do?

(e) Someone in your class is giving a party. Everyone has been invited except you. What can you do?

(f) You forgot about an important appointment with your boss (teacher/great-uncle) and have just realised that you should have met him two hours ago at the 'Peking Restaurant'. What can you do?

More problems and moral dilemmas can be found in the problem pages of magazines.

Remarks The students should learn to work beyond the obvious alternatives.

(Idea adapted from de Bono 1973.)

91 Viewpoints

Aims	*Skills* – speaking
	Language – all elements
	Other – empathy, role taking
Level	Intermediate
Organisation	Groups of three to five students
Preparation	As many handouts as there are groups (see Part 2)

Time   15–20 minutes

Procedure   *Step 1:* The teacher divides the class into small groups and presents the situation:

Mary Taylor, a 35 year-old housewife, would like to go back to her job, teaching physics and mathematics, after an eight year break. Imagine what her husband, her eight year-old daughter, her mother-in-law, her parents and the headmaster might feel about the situation.

The teacher writes the names, ages and jobs of the people mentioned in the situation on the board and assigns one of these people to each group. The students discuss amongst themselves what they think this particular person might feel. The group secretary in each group makes some notes.

Step 2: The teacher gives each group that part of the handout which concerns 'their' person (see Part 2). The groups compare their own ideas with those on the handout. They then try to add more thoughts and arguments.

Step 3: One person from each group comes forward. These students sit in a circle in the middle of the class and hold a conversation in which they put their arguments and feelings forward. The 'fishbowl' procedure (see Introduction, p. 9) is followed.

Variations   *1:* Step 1 is omitted.

2: Commercially produced materials for role play (e.g. Lynch 1977 and Menné 1975) may be used.

3: The students devise their own problem situations.

3.5 Problem-solving activities

Activity	Topic type	Level	Organis- ation	Prep- aration	Time in minutes
92 Desert island (2)	fact.	int.	indiv./pairs/ groups	no	10–20
93 Rescue	fact.	int./adv.	groups	no	10–20
94 Desperate decision	fact.	int./adv.	groups	Part 2	30–40
95 Fire	pers./fact.	beg./int.	indiv.	no	5–10
96 One day in London	pers./fact.	int.	pairs	no	15–20
97 Our room	pers./fact.	int.	pairs	Part 2	15–20
98 Treasure hunt	fact.	int.	indiv./pairs/ groups/class	yes	days
99 Something for everybody	pers./fact.	int./adv.	groups/class	no	10–20
100 Group holiday	pers./fact.	int.	groups	Part 2	15–20
101 Everyday problems	pers./fact.	int.	groups/class	no	10–15
102 Friendly Biscuits Inc.	fact	int.	groups	Part 2	10–20
103 Baker Street	fact.	int.	class	Part 2	5–15
104 Problem page (1)	fact.	int.	pairs/groups	Part 2	20–30
105 Problem page (2)	fact./pers.	int./adv.	indiv./class	Part 2	20–30

pers. = personal; fact. = factual; beg. = beginners; int. = intermediate; adv. = advanced; indiv. = individuals; groups = small groups; pairs = two people working together; class = everybody working together; Part 2 = material for the exercise is to be found in Part 2.

In the following activities the learners have to find solutions to various types of problem. In the case of puzzles like No. 103 *Baker Street* there is just one correct solution: however, most of the exercises in this section lead to a discussion of several ways of solving the problems. The problem tasks themselves range from the imaginary (e.g. No. 92 *Desert island (2)* or No. 93 *Rescue*) to the more realistic (e.g. No. 97 *Our room* or No. 99 *Something for everybody*). The latter provide situations which the learners might conceivably have to face outside the classroom.

Apart from the activities focusing on the likes and dislikes of individual learners, which therefore need an initial phase where each student works on his own, most of the problem-solving tasks in this section require pair or group work throughout. In some ways these activities are similar to ranking exercises (section 3.1) because, like them, they generate discussions of the importance or relevance of statements, ideas or procedures. But unlike ranking exercises, problem-solving activities demand that the learners themselves decide upon the items to be ranked. Thus there is more creative use of the foreign language. It is advisable to use the less complex ranking exercises before any problem-solving activities if the students have not done this kind of work before.

The language which is needed for problem-solving activities depends on the topic of each exercise, but in general students will have to make suggestions, give reasons, and accept, modify or reject suggestions and reasons given by others. Puzzles like No. 103 *Baker Street* practise question forms.

More problem-solving activities are listed in sections 2.4 (Jigsaw tasks) and 3.1 (Ranking exercises). Further suggestions can be found in Fletcher and Birt 1979 and Krupar 1973.

92 Desert island (2)

Aims   *Skills* – speaking, writing
Language – giving and asking for reasons, agreeing and disagreeing, making suggestions
Other – imagination, common sense, fun

Level   Intermediate

Organisation   Individuals, pairs, groups

Preparation   None

Time   10–20 minutes

Procedure   *Step 1:* The teacher describes the task to the students: 'You are stranded on a desert island a long way from anywhere. There is a fresh water spring on the island, and there are banana trees and coconut palms. The climate is mild. Make a list of eight to twelve things which you think are necessary for survival.'
Students work on their own.

Step 2: Students pair up and compare lists. They agree on a common list of a maximum of ten items.

Step 3: The students discuss the new lists in groups of four to six students. They decide on a group list of a maximum of eight items and rank these according to their importance.

Variations   See No. 50 *Desert island (1)*.

93 Rescue

Aims	*Skills* – speaking *Language* –stating an opinion, giving and asking for reasons, agreeing and disagreeing, comparisons *Other* – thinking about one's values
Level	Intermediate/advanced
Organisation	Groups of five to eight students
Preparation	None
Time	10–20 minutes
Procedure	*Step 1:* The teacher explains the situation: 'The Earth is doomed. All life is going to perish in two days due to radiation. A spaceship from another solar system lands and offers to rescue twelve people, who could start a new world on an empty planet very much like Earth. Imagine you are the selection committee and you have to decide who may be rescued. Think of a list of criteria which you would use in your decision.' 　　*Step 2:* Each group discusses the problem and tries to work out a list. 　　*Step 3:* Each group presents its list of criteria to the class. The lists are discussed.
Variations	The task can be made more specific, e.g. 'Find ten criteria. You can award up to 100 points if a candidate gets full marks on all counts, e.g. appearance 5, intelligence 30, fertility 15, physical fitness 20, etc.
Remarks	Although the basic problem is a rather depressing one, it helps students to clarify their own values as regards judging others.

94 Desperate decision

Aims	*Skills* – reading comprehension, speaking *Language* – making suggestions, stating possibilities, agreeing and disagreeing *Other* – imagination
Level	Intermediate/advanced
Organisation	Groups of three to six students each
Preparation	A handout for each student (see Part 2)
Time	30–40 minutes
Procedure	*Step 1:* Each student receives a handout (Part 2) and reads the description of the situation. Comprehension difficulties are

cleared up, and the teacher may ask a few comprehension
questions (e.g. How many of the hiking group are feeling ill?
How many can read a map?).

Step 2: The groups try and find as many courses of action
as possible. They should write them down. Then they discuss
the advantages and disadvantages of each solution and decide
on the best one. Again they should write down the reasons
for their choice.

Step 3: Each group presents its solution. The other groups
should challenge the arguments and conclusions of the
reporting group.

Variations   If a solution cannot be agreed on within the group, the
students can try and work out a role play. Each student takes
over the part of one of the people in the task and argues from
that person's point of view.

95   Fire

Aims	*Skills* – speaking
	Language – asking for and giving reasons, conditional
	Other – thinking about essentials
Level	Beginners/intermediate
Organisation	Individuals
Preparation	None
Time	5–10 minutes
Procedure	*Step 1:* The teacher describes the situation to the class:

'A fire has broken out where you live. You have a few
minutes to grab five of your belongings and rescue them.
Which five things would you take? Remember, you have to
carry them all.'

Step 2: Each student writes down up to five things he
would rescue from the fire.

Step 3: Some students read out their lists and explain why
they would take these things. The others should ask questions
like 'Why wouldn't you take . . .? What about your . . .?'

Variations   A different situation may be chosen:
'You are staying on your own in a holiday cottage in Scotland
for three months next summer. The cottage is miles away
from any village or farm. It has electricity and water and a big
store of food. The sea is not far away and there is also a trout
stream and a small forest. Which things (e.g. radio, books,
musical instruments, materials and equipment for hobbies

and sports) would you need to survive the three months without being bored?'
Each student makes a list of all the things he would like to take with him. A few students then report back to the class. The most commonly chosen and the most unusual objects can be found out.

96 One day in London

Aims	*Skills* – speaking
	Language – all elements
	Other – cooperation
Level	Intermediate
Organisation	Pairs
Preparation	None
Time	15–20 minutes
Procedure	*Step 1:* The teacher describes the situation:

'You have to plan how to spend a day in London with your partner. Both of you arrive at Heathrow airport at 9 a.m. and you have to be back at the airport at 9 p.m. There is a self-drive car which you may use. It has a full tank. You receive £10 each, but you have no other money. Decide what you would like to do. You should plan the day in such a way that you are happy with it.'

Step 2: The students work in pairs. The partners find out from each other what they would like to do and what they would not like to do. They then work out a timetable for the day.

Step 3: The students report their plans back to the class. Similarities and differences between individual suggestions are discussed.

Step 4: (*optional*) The teacher asks how the timetables were agreed on. Did one partner dominate? Did one partner try to persuade the other one? Was there a lot of arguing? Did one of the pair have to give up a lot of ideas? Who made the suggestions? etc.

Variations	In connection with other work done in class (e.g. texts studied), different locations (New York, Sydney, etc.) can be chosen.

97 Our room

Aims   *Skills* – speaking
Language – all elements (especially items of furniture,
prepositions, adverbial phrases)
Other – cooperation

Level   Intermediate

Organisation   Pairs

Preparation   A handout for each student (see Part 2), scissors for each pair
of students, a transparency for the overhead projector with
the floor-plan of the room, overhead projector

Time   15–20 minutes

Procedure   *Step 1:* Each student receives a handout. Together with his
partner he tries to furnish the room using the pieces of
furniture available on the handout. Both partners discuss
which pieces of furniture to choose and where to put them.
Each item on the list has been allocated a certain number of
points. They must not use up more than 100 points
furnishing the room. In order to make the furnishing more
realistic, the pieces of furniture may be cut out of the handout
and placed on the plan of the room. In doing so the students
practise sentences like: 'Shall we put the bed next to the
window or in the corner? We could put the bookcases near
the writing table. If the wardrobe is put at right angles to the
wall then the bed is in a small alcove.'

Step 2: Some students explain their arrangement of the
furniture by placing their cut-outs on the plan on the
overhead projector and answering questions as to the reasons
behind their decisions.

Variations   *1:* Students can also decide about a colour scheme for their
room, e.g. 'You may choose the furniture and up to four of
the following colours for your room. At the moment the
room has white walls and a dark brown carpet. These are the
colours: light brown, red, purple, light blue, dark blue, dark
green, maroon, yellow, grey, black, orange, pink.'

2: The task can be varied by presenting the students with
coloured catalogues from furniture shops from which they
cut out the pieces of furniture they would like.

107

98 Treasure hunt

Aims	*Skills* – all four skills
	Language – all elements
	Other – fun, individualised learning
Level	Intermediate
Organisation	Individuals, pairs, groups and class
Preparation	See Procedure
Time	A few minutes each lesson for a number of days (or weeks)
Procedure	*General remarks:* All the tasks for the treasure hunt have to be worked out in advance. Ideally the tasks should be tailor-made for individual students, so that their strengths may be exploited or their special talents used. The basic principle of a treasure hunt is as follows. Each student has to follow instructions and fulfil a certain task. If he does it properly he is rewarded with a piece of information, e.g. a word or letter. All the pieces of information collected by the students have to be combined to find the general solution, i.e. the treasure. (There is a simple version of this type of activity in No. 37 *Jigsaw guessing*.) It would be useful (if possible) to enlist the help of other English-speaking people so that the tasks for the students can include phoning and letter writing. The prize for finding the solution can be anything from a bag of sweets to a visit to an English film. The teacher who knows her class will have lots of ideas about what to choose.

Possible tasks (These are suggestions which should be adapted for individual classes.)

(a) There is a poem on page xx in your textbook. Learn it by heart and recite it in the next lesson. You will then get an envelope from your teacher. (Envelope: Your word is: *you*)

(b) (For two students) Here are the lines of a dialogue, all mixed up. Put them in the right order and write your own ending to the dialogue. Act it in front of the class in the next lesson. You will then get an envelope from your teacher. (Envelope: Your word is: *surprise*)

(c) Here is a text where some words are spelt wrongly. Check with your dictionary to find out the correct spelling. Write down all the letters that were wrong. They make a word. Ask Mrs B if you have found the correct word. (Word: *there*)

(d) Phone this number xxx–xxxx and ask to speak to Mr Z. Find out where he spent his holiday last year, tell him about yours. If you don't make any mistakes he will tell you the next word. (Word: *is*)

(e) Read this story and tell the class what it is about in the next lesson. Your teacher will give you the next word. (Word: *cupboard*)

(f) Here are the rules for a new game. Together with students C and D make the materials for the game, so that we can play it next week. Your teacher will give you the next word. (Word: *for*)

(g) Go and explain the new game to class X. Play it with them. You will then get the next word from their teacher. (Word: *a*)

(h) Write a letter to Mrs Y. Ask her for the recipe for trifle. If your letter has no mistakes she will send you the recipe. The word you need is underlined with a red pen in the recipe. Give the recipe to E, F and G. (Word: *in*)

(i) Record the news on an English-language radio programme on Monday and write down the text. Bring the recording and the text with you to the lesson on Thursday. Your teacher will tell you the next word. (Word: *the*)

Solution: There is a surprise for you in the cupboard.

When the teacher has worked out the tasks they can be given to the students one by one. Progress in finding the solution can be marked on a special notice on the wall in the classroom. In an English-language environment the possibilities for tasks are, of course, far greater than abroad. The main point is, though, to adapt the tasks to the individual students and make them practise skills which they will need later on (e.g. looking words up in a dictionary, following instructions, etc.) or which are suited to their interests and capabilities.

99 Something for everybody

Aims	*Skills* – speaking *Language* – making suggestions, expressing likes, dislikes and preferences, giving in *Other* – cooperation
Level	Intermediate/advanced
Organisation	Groups, class

Preparation	None
Time	10–20 minutes
Procedure	*Step 1:* The students form groups and the teacher describes the situation:

'Imagine that you, that is all of you together, have £20 left over from a bargain sale you organised. You should now think of what you could do with the money so that everyone in the class is satisfied. First write down all the ideas you have without talking about them or commenting on them, then rank them. When you have found one suggestion you all agree with, present it to the class.'

    Step 2: Each group presents its suggestion. The class then tries to agree on a common proposal by arguing and presenting reasons (not by majority vote!).

Remarks	See No. 87 *Brainstorming* and No. 46 *Rank order* for descriptions of these procedures.

100 Group holiday

Aims	*Skills* – speaking
	Language – asking for and giving reasons, agreeing and disagreeing, making suggestions, giving in
	Other – fair discussion
Level	Intermediate
Organisation	Groups of five to seven students
Preparation	A handout for each student (see Part 2)
Time	15–20 minutes
Procedure	*Step 1:* The class is divided into groups. Each student receives a handout containing eight suggestions for a two week holiday. Each group now has to find the one holiday that they would like to have *together*. A decision should be reached by discussion and finding good arguments and not by a majority vote. If the group really cannot agree on a type of holiday they would all like to share, they may present their case to the class for further discussion. Groups may also suggest a kind of holiday not mentioned in the handout.

    Step 2: Each group describes the holiday they have chosen and outlines the reason for this choice. The other groups may ask questions or comment.

Variations	As a follow-up exercise the students can be asked to rank a number of pictures taken from travel brochures. Criteria for ranking may be the interest stimulated by the photos or the degree of adventure inherent in them.

Remarks   A class discussion as to what students expect from a holiday can follow.

101   Everyday problems

Aims   *Skills* – listening comprehension, speaking
Language – describing something, making suggestions, discussing alternatives
Other – helping each other, empathy
Level   Intermediate
Organisation   Groups of six to eight students or class
Preparation   None
Time   10–15 minutes
Procedure   Individual students describe a problem they have, e.g. always forgetting their keys, not being able to remember names, oversleeping, etc. The others try to suggest ways and means of helping with the problem.
Remarks   A supportive atmosphere is necessary so that students do not feel embarrassed or harassed.

102   Friendly Biscuits Inc.

Aims   *Skills* – speaking, listening comprehension
Language – asking for information
Other – cooperation
Level   Intermediate
Organisation   Four groups of students
Preparation   A different handout for each group (see Part 2)
Time   10–20 minutes
Procedure   *Step 1:* The class is divided into four groups. Each group has to find the answers to these questions:
How many men and women work in the management of Friendly Biscuits Inc.?
What are their names and jobs?
Each group receives a different handout (see Part 2) which contains only a quarter of the necessary information. The groups have five minutes to decide which pieces of information they need and how they can organise their search for more information. Writing things down is only allowed at each group's 'home table'. Members of different groups must not show each other their group handout.

111

Step 2: The groups have five minutes to interview members of other groups in order to find the answers. The teacher should stress the two rules again: No writing except at the 'home table' of each group. No showing of the handout.

Step 3: After five minutes everyone returns to his group, where all the information is collected. The answers to the questions are written down and handed to the teacher.

Step 4: The teacher announces which answers are correct.

Variations   Instead of grouping the students at the beginning, this can be done by the students themselves, when each of them has received a handout.

Remarks   In large classes there could be two groups of each kind (A, B, C and D).

Solution:
FRIENDLY BISCUITS INC.

Board of directors:	Ron Preedy	Brenda Pilot	David Parsons
Personal assistants:	Mary Hill	Angela Woodhouse	Philippa Gordon
Secretaries:	Carole Ward	John Martin	Jean Carter
Typists:	Sheila Rogers	Christina Stead	Roger Haldane

four men, eight women

103   Baker Street

Aims	*Skills* – speaking
	Language – all elements
	Other – cooperation
Level	Intermediate
Organisation	Class
Preparation	One copy of the handout (see Part 2) cut into strips (if there are more than 20 students two copies of the handout should be cut up)
Time	5–15 minutes
Procedure	*Step 1:* The teacher draws the following diagram on the board or overhead projector.

The situation is outlined to the students:
'These are five houses in Baker Street. One person lives in each house. The aim is to find out each person's name, whether he or she is married or not, what pet he or she owns, which books he or she likes and what he or she likes to drink.

	12	14	16	18	20
Name					
Marital status					
Pet					
Book					
Drink					

Each of you will get a piece of paper with some information on it. Share what you know and try to fill in the table.'

Step 2: Each student receives his strip of paper. It should be left entirely to the students how they organise the collection of information. The teacher's sole function is to remind the students to use English, should that be necessary.

Remarks   If there are fewer than 20 students, each student should receive two strips.

This activity is built on the jigsaw principle. For more jigsaw exercises see section 2.4.

104 Problem page (1)

Aims   *Skills* – reading comprehension, speaking
Language – all elements
Other – empathy

Level   Intermediate

Organisation   Pairs or groups

Preparation   Two handouts (see Part 2; one per student of 104A, one per pair or group of 104B)

Time   20–30 minutes

Procedure   *Step 1:* Each student receives a handout. The pairs or groups decide which letter they would like to discuss. They talk about the problem described in the letter and suggest ways of solving it. One of the pair or a group secretary makes some notes.

Step 2: Each secretary reports on the problem and the suggested solution.

Step 3: Each pair or group receives the handout with the answers. They talk about the advice given in the answers.

Variations   *1:* Each group is allotted a particular letter.

2: All groups are given the same letter.

3: Every group has to discuss all the letters.

4: Half of the groups receive the letters and have to guess at the answers, the other half get the answers and have to guess what the problems are.

Remarks   Problem pages can be found in many women's and teenagers' magazines.

105   Problem page (2)

Aims   *Skills* – reading comprehension, speaking, writing
Language – all elements
Other – empathy

Level   Intermediate/advanced

Organisation   Individuals, class

Preparation   A handout (see Part 2) per student and three coloured dots or stickers per student

Time   20–30 minutes

Procedure   *Step 1:* Each student receives a copy of the handout with the letters on and is asked to write a reply to one of them.

Step 2: All the replies are put up on the wall so that everybody can read them. If there are letters which say almost the same thing, only one of these is left up. Each student is given three stickers (coloured dots). He should stick these on the letters which he agrees with most of all. He can use all three dots on one letter or spread them out.

Step 3: The three letters ranked most highly in this way are read out and discussed in class.

Step 4: They can be compared with the answers given by the magazine on the other handout.

4 Stories and scenes

4.1 Miming

Activity	Topic type	Level	Organis-ation	Prep-aration	Time in minutes
106 Adverb charade	fact.	beg./int.	pairs/class	yes	10–15
107 Miming people and objects	fact./pers.	beg.	indiv./pairs/ groups	yes	10–15
108 Daily life	fact./pers.	beg./int.	groups	yes	15–20
109 Hotel receptionist	fact.	int.	class/groups	yes	15–20
110 Messages	fact.	int.	pairs	yes	15–20

pers. = personal; fact. = factual; beg. = beginners; int. = intermediate; indiv. = individuals; groups = small groups; pairs = two people working together; class = everybody working together.

Objects, actions or people have to be mimed and guessed in the following five activities. The mimes are done in pairs or groups; in one case individual students have to perform their mimes for the whole class. Shy students or students not used to this kind of activity may not find it easy to act something out in front of everyone else. This should be kept in mind when you do mimes for the first time with your class. Pair or group work reduces stage fright to a certain extent and can be used as a starter. Since the speed of the guessing depends on the quality of the mime, less inventive students may not be such popular performers as others.

In spite of these possible drawbacks, miming activities are valuable language-learning situations. Guessing something is linked with the real desire to find out and thus is a true communicative situation (see introduction to section 2.3). Furthermore, miming exercises train the students' skill of observation and improvisation. Finally, miming exercises are useful because they emphasise the importance of gesture and facial expression in communication. In terms of language elements, they practise question forms and expressing possibilities.

Language-learning exercises using mime are to be found in

Dixey and Rinvolucri 1978, Dubin and Margol 1977, Maley and Duff 1978.

106 Adverb charade

Aims	*Skills* – speaking
	Language – asking yes/no questions, adverbs
	Other – fun
Level	Beginners/intermediate
Organisation	Pairs, class
Preparation	About 50 small pieces of paper
Time	10–15 minutes
Procedure	*Step 1:* The pieces of paper are distributed, so that each student receives two. On one piece of paper he writes a simple action, e.g. eating a banana, knitting, reading a paper; on the other an adverb, e.g. angrily, badly, cautiously, etc. All the pieces of paper are put in two piles face down.
	Step 2: Each student teams up with a partner. The first pair of students come to the front of the class. One draws a piece of paper from the action pile, the other from the adverb pile. Both mime their action in the manner described by the adverb. The rest of the class guess.
Variations	This can be played as a competitive team game.

107 Miming people and objects

Aims	*Skills* – speaking
	Language – making conjectures, asking questions
	Other – observation, fun
Level	Beginners
Organisation	Individuals, pairs, groups
Preparation	Several piles of small pieces of paper with descriptions of people (e.g. an old man, a fat bus conductor), names of objects, photos or drawings of people and objects
Time	10–15 minutes
Procedure	Instructions as to what the students have to mime are given verbally or visually. The individual mimes can be organised in one of the following ways:
	(a) Every student chooses a piece of paper from a pile and mimes the person or the object. The others guess.

(b) Two or three students combine their miming tasks to mime a short scene together. The others observe and make suggestions about the people and objects in the mime.

(c) Each group of students is given the same people and objects to mime. Performances and different realisations are discussed.

(d) Chain mime. One student starts by miming his object/person. Another student joins him until up to ten students are involved in miming a situation.

Remarks   The number of variations for mimes is probably infinite and there is plenty of scope for the creative teacher.

108 Daily life

Aims   *Skills* – speaking, writing
Language – asking questions, stating one's opinions, making suggestions, agreeing and disagreeing
Other – observation, fun

Level   Beginners/intermediate

Organisation   Groups of three to five students

Preparation   Short dialogues on separate pieces of paper, some objects as props

Time   15–20 minutes

Procedure   *Step 1:* Each group of students receives a different dialogue and has five minutes in which to organise the miming. They decide who takes which role, and what props are needed.

Step 2: Each group performs their mime in turn. After each performance the students in the audience suggest what the mime was about.

Variations   *1:* Each group may speak just one sentence of the dialogue during the mime.

2: (For advanced students) During each mime the students in the audience make notes on the topic and roles. When they have watched all the mimes they argue within their groups and try to work out a list of all the topics/roles in the mimes.

Remarks   Suitable dialogues can be found in textbooks.

109 Hotel receptionist

Aims *Skills* – speaking (reading comprehension)
Language – all kinds of questions, expressing understanding, asking for confirmation
Other – observation, fun

Level Intermediate

Organisation Class, groups of five to eight students

Preparation At least as many messages as there are students, on small slips of paper

Time 15–20 minutes

Procedure *Step 1:* The teacher explains the situation.
'The setting is a hotel in an English-speaking country. A guest staying at the hotel has a very bad cold and has lost his voice. He therefore has to communicate with the hotel receptionist by miming.'
In the first two or three rounds the teacher takes the part of the hotel receptionist. The guest is played by one of the students. This student draws a slip of paper with a message on (e.g. It's very cold in my room. I can't turn the radiators on. Could you send someone up to have a look?) and, playing the part of the guest, mimes his request while the hotel receptionist guesses (e.g. Are you cold? No? I see your room is cold. Have you tried to turn on the heating? etc.). The rest of the class should help the teacher (receptionist) figure out the request. The receptionist's task is finished when he has found out the exact message. (In the example given above the statement: 'You are cold and the heating is not on' would not be enough.)
  Step 2: The students are divided into groups. The members of each group sit in a circle and take turns to play the guest and the hotel receptionist. Each group has a supply of messages to draw from.

Variations *1:* The setting is changed to a Lost Property Office where students have to claim objects they have lost. The objects are written on small pieces of paper.
  2: In addition to miming, drawing may be allowed.

Possible messages I have to catch an early train tomorrow. Could I be woken at 5.30 a.m., please?
I am going out now. I am expecting a phone call from my wife. Could you please tell her that I've lost my voice and have written a letter to her?
I have forgotten the number of my room.

Where is the nearest post office?

Can you get two opera tickets for tomorrow night? But only if there are seats in the first fifteen rows.

Can you change a £5 note into 10p pieces?

I'd like to go on a sightseeing tour round the town tomorrow. When do they leave? How long do they take and how much do they cost?

Is there a heated indoor swimming pool in the town? How far is it?

Somebody has put a crocodile in my bath. Please come quickly.

There's a very funny noise coming from the room next to mine. I'm afraid that somebody might be ill.

Remarks   (See Maley and Duff 1978.)

110 Messages

Aims   *Skills* – writing, speaking
Language – expressing one's opinions, making conjectures, saying something is right/wrong
Other – fun

Level   Intermediate

Organisation   Pairs

Preparation   As many pieces of paper with messages on as there are students

Time   15–20 minutes

Procedure   *Step 1:* Each student takes a message which he is not allowed to show to anybody else in the class. Then the students find a partner.

Step 2: All the students stand around the walls of the classroom making sure that their partner is as far away as possible. The first student in each pair mimes his message to his partner. That is, half of the class are miming, while the other half are watching. The observing partners write down the message as they interpret it. Then the second students in each pair mime their messages.

Step 3: Everyone sits down with his partner and tells him what he thought the message was. Then the original messages are read out.

Possible   I'd like to go to the cinema with you. Meet me at my house at
messages   7 p.m.

Can I borrow your record player? Mine is broken.
I am having a party on Saturday. Can you come?
Could we do our homework together this afternoon?
I am going to go shopping tomorrow to get a new bicycle. Do you want to come?
Please do some shopping for me. Get four pounds of apples, two bottles of lemonade and some toilet paper.
I found a red purse on the floor. It has £2.50 in it. Is it yours?
Go to the library and get a book on cats.
Your trousers have split.
There is a big white stain on your pullover. It's right under your left arm.

4.2 Role play and simulations

Activity	Topic type	Level	Organis- ation	Prep- aration	Time in minutes
111 Telephoning	fact.	int./adv.	pairs	Part 2	15–20
112 TV interview	fact.	int./adv.	groups	no	20–30
113 Talk show	fact./pers.	int./adv.	groups/class	yes	45–90
114 Controversy in the school	fact.	int./adv.	groups/class	Part 2	20–45
115 The XY society	fact.	int./adv.	groups/teams class	no	5–8 hrs.
116 Swap shop	fact./pers.	int.	indiv.	yes	20–30
117 Interview for a job	fact.	int.	groups	yes	30–45
118 Making a radio programme	fact.	int./adv.	pairs/groups/	yes	3–5 hrs.

pers. = personal; fact. = factual; int. = intermediate; indiv. = individuals; groups = small groups; pairs = two people working together; class = everybody working together; Part 2 = material for the exercise is to be found in Part 2.

It is not easy to distinguish clearly between role play and simulation. Both are forms of games mirroring a slice of reality. As a rule simulations are more highly structured and contain more diverse elements in their content and procedure. 'Simulations are simplified patterns of human interactions or social processes where the players participate in roles' (Davison and Gordon 1978, p. 55). Most simulations demand that the participants are supplied with background information and materials to work from both before and during the simulation. Accomplishing the task set in a simulation has sometimes got to be done within a time limit, e.g. in writing the front page of a newspaper, just as in reality.

In contrast to simulations, role plays often consist of short scenes, which can be realistic – as in acting out a shopping situation – or pure fantasy – as in pretending to interview a Martian on TV. Realistic role plays have been common features of situational language teaching for a long time and are catered for by suitable dialogues in most beginners' textbooks. Also a lot of materials for role play have been published (see Heyworth 1978, Lynch 1977, Menné 1975, Seely 1978, Walker 1979). Role plays may be enacted around everyday situations as well as around topical problems like the generation gap or vandalism. My choice of role plays and

121

simulations was guided by the intention to achieve effective language learning situations rather than extremely original topics. The role plays and simulations included here should also encourage teachers to develop their own materials.

The materials necessary for a simulation should be more varied and complex to suit the multi-layered structure of a simulation. This does not mean that simulations cannot be adapted to suit the needs and interests of your students. Both No. 115 *The XY society* and No. 118 *Making a radio programme* can easily be changed in their topical outline while keeping to the procedure given for each activity.

Role plays make use of two types of materials, *role cards* and *cue cards*. The worksheet for No. 111 *Telephoning* contains cue cards, which guide the players as to what they should say in detail. For exercise No. 117 *Interview for a job* Part 2 contains role cards, which tell the players what the person whose role they are taking is like, but leaves them free to express themselves without restrictions. (Another example of cue cards is to be found in No. 45 *Question and answer cards*.)

Role plays are quite demanding foreign language situations in that the players have to use the foreign language correctly and adequately both in terms of the foreign language itself and the particular role that is acted out. Even very advanced learners of English are rarely able to speak consciously in a particular style or register, which may be necessary for a role. For these students the study of texts, or better, video tapes of encounters where the foreign language is used at different levels of formality, can be a valuable training in this skill prior to role play.

Role plays improve the students' oral performance generally, and simulations quite often train all four skills. The complexity of simulations, which run over several stages, prevents the teacher from exactly determining beforehand which structures, words and language skills will be needed by the players. Therefore simulations mainly constitute practice sessions where the participants draw on everything they have learnt so far.

A number of activities in this book may be complemented by role plays, e.g. Nos. 104 and 105 *Problem page* (1) and (2). A great number of articles and books have been published on the use of role plays, and the following titles are only a small selection: British Council 1977, Dixey and Rinvolucri 1978, Fletcher and Birt 1979, Heyworth 1978, Lynch 1977, Maley and Duff 1978, Menné 1975, Seely 1978;

on simulations: Davison and Gordon 1978, *Learning for
Change* 1977, Taylor and Walford 1978; on simulations in
foreign language teaching: British Council 1977, Herbert and
Sturtridge 1979, Jones 1982.

111 Telephoning

Aims	*Skills* – speaking (writing) *Language* – insisting, interrupting, directing the conversation, hesitating, expressing uncertainty *Other* – improvisation, flexibility in using the foreign language
Level	Intermediate/advanced
Organisation	Pairs
Preparation	Role cards (see Part 2)
Time	15–20 minutes
Procedure	*Step 1:* The class is divided into two teams (A and B) and each team into sub-groups of three to five students. Each A-group receives a copy of an A-role card, each B-group a copy of a B-role card (see Part 2). The students in each group work out some phrases which they could use in the telephone conversation indicated on the role card. *Step 2:* One person from an A-group and one from a B-group act the telephone conversation in front of the group. Up to four more pairs give their version as well. This procedure is repeated with different role cards.
Variations	With advanced students the preparation phase may be shorter, i.e. two students draw an A-role card and a B-role card, respectively, think of what they could say for one minute and then act the telephone conversation.

112 TV interview

Aims	*Skills* – speaking, writing *Language* – describing something, (present simple) questions, introducing someone *Other* – thinking about the ideal family
Level	Intermediate/advanced
Organisation	Groups of four to six students
Preparation	None
Time	20–30 minutes

Procedure *Step 1:* One of the groups has to prepare the role of the interviewer and write down questions the interviewer could ask the members of the 'ideal family'. All the other groups represent an 'ideal family'; they should allocate the different roles within the group and talk about the personalities, ways of behaviour and ideas of the people in their ideal family.

Step 2: Each ideal family is interviewed by a different interviewer in turn in front of the class. At the beginning of the role play each member of the family introduces either himself or another family member.

Step 3: Since a lot of the students' values and ideals regarding families will have become obvious, they should be discussed afterwards.

Variations Other ideal groups can be interviewed, e.g. 'ideal holiday group', 'ideal flat-sharing group'.

113 Talk show

Aims *Skills* – speaking
Language – introducing somebody, describing one's job/hobby, asking all kinds of questions
Other – imagination, fun

Level Intermediate/advanced
Organisation Groups, class
Preparation Video equipment (optional)
Time 45–90 minutes
Procedure *Step 1:* There are three alternatives as to how the talk show can be organised:

(a) The students play themselves; then the activity belongs to the warming-up category and students talk in order to get to know each other better. Each student writes his name on a piece of paper.

(b) The students write out role cards for fictitious people, which are shuffled and handed out.

(c) Each student designs his own role card. They should all follow the same pattern, e.g.

| Name: | Country: | Job: |
| Age: | Married/children: | Hobbies: |

One group of four to six students prepare three topics each and suitable questions as talk masters of the show.

Step 2: Each talk master is allotted about the same number of people to interview (there should not be more than five interviews per talk master). Each talk master draws a certain number of role cards or name cards (if every student plays himself) from the general pile. Each talk master tells his group which topics he wants to ask them about and how he is going to interview them.

Step 3: Each group, consisting of one talk master and up to five people being interviewed, acts out their talk show in front of the class. The rest of the class are the audience and may write down additional questions or suggestions regarding the topic, the people being interviewed or the talk master himself. The talk show is interrupted after ten minutes, and the questions from the audience read out and answered. Then it is the turn of the next group to present their talk show.

If video equipment is available, the talk shows can be recorded and discussed at a later stage or shown to other classes.

Remarks   Letting each group perform could lead to boredom in big classes. One could either decide on two or three groups by lot or space the performances out and call on one group per week.

114   Controversy in the school

Aims   *Skills* – all four skills
         Language – all elements
         Other – cooperation
Level   Intermediate/advanced
Organisation   Groups, class
Preparation   Handouts (see Part 2)
Time   20–45 minutes
Procedure   *Step 1:* Each student receives a handout. All the texts are read and language difficulties cleared up.

Step 2: Students are then divided into groups. One group prepares arguments the parents might put forward, another group thinks of the point of view of the pupils concerned. All in all there can be up to eight different groups, dealing with the parents, teachers, principal (headmaster), pupils of different age groups, local press and school administration (local education authority). The groups arrange meetings, e.g. the parents want to talk to the headmaster, the local press interview teachers and pupils, etc.

Step 3: The final step can be a panel discussion with a representative of each group on the panel.
Variations   *1:* Instead of arranging meetings each group can produce a leaflet/poster outlining their position.

125

2: All kinds of issues can be dealt with in this type of activity, e.g. pollution control, campaigning for a new play-group/playground, fighting against a new motorway, etc.

Remarks (Idea adapted from *Learning for Change* 1977.)

115 The XY society

Aims	*Skills* – all four skills
	Language – all language elements
	Other – fun
Level	Intermediate/advanced
Organisation	Groups, teams, class
Preparation	None
Time	5–8 hours
Procedure	The activity follows the steps outlined in the diagram below. The first step involves agreeing on the aim of the society to be founded and naming it. The society can have a

Society activity	Classroom activity	Structures and vocabulary
A Meeting to found a society	Discussion of aims	Present simple and continuous, We'd like to . . ., We'll . . ., We have to . . .
B Election of office bearers	Election of chairperson, secretary, treasurer and the committee	nominate, second, ballot, majority, deals with . . .
C Agenda for a forthcoming meeting	Drawing up an agenda	I propose/suggest . . ., dates, numbers
D Items on the agenda: fund-raising, publicity, demonstration	Debate, note taking, letter writing, finding a motto, designing posters	. . . should . . ., . . . could . . ., . . . might . . .
E Rules	Discussion	Members will have to . . ., . . . must never . . .
F Membership forms and cards	Devising and designing application form and membership card	Have you ever been to . . .? Are you married . . .? Names?

Further activities: preparation of newsletter, radio or TV programme about the society.

'nonsense purpose' like making trousers the compulsory dress for everyone (Trouser Society) or a real one like founding a debating club at school (Debating Society). It will largely depend on the students' and teacher's interests which type of society is chosen.

Variations Any of the steps from the table can be tackled on its own. The students are then given the information which is necessary, e.g. if the teacher wants them to practise writing skills Step D is appropriate. The students would then have to be told the name and purpose of the society.

Remarks (Idea adapted from Syed 1978.)

116 Swap shop

Aims *Skills* – speaking
Language – offering something, expressing interest, describing adjectives, if-clauses
Other – fun swapping things

Level Intermediate

Organisation Individuals

Preparation Role cards (see Procedure), cards with descriptions or drawings of suitable objects (about three cards per student)

Time 20–30 minutes

Procedure *Step 1:* Each student receives a role card (e.g. You are a collector of model trains; you are especially interested in steam engines   Or: You are a fan of the Beatles and are desperately looking for a copy of their white album in good condition, because your own copy is very badly scratched) and two or three object cards (e.g. The Beatles white album, sleeve is very torn, records in passable condition   Or: Model of the French high speed train   Or: Victorian doll; one arm missing; real hair).

Step 2: The students walk around and try to find others who are either interested in one of the objects they have to offer or who can offer them something.

Variations Real objects can be brought along and used for this activity.

Remarks Care should be taken that there are several suitable objects for the individual collectors so that finding partners for a swap is not too difficult. Students should be told beforehand that it might be necessary to swap with more than one person.

117 Interview for a job

Aims	*Skills* – speaking
	Language – asking questions, stating one's intentions, giving information about oneself
	Other – preparation for possible real life situation
Level	Intermediate
Organisation	Five groups
Preparation	A handout for each group (see Part 2 No. 53 *Looking for a job*)
Time	30–45 minutes
Procedure	*Step 1:* The class is divided into five groups. One group represents Lindon Borough Council, each of the four remaining groups, one of the four applicants. Lindon Borough Council group receive the full handout; each of the other groups get the advertisements and their own application.
	Step 2: The Borough Council group work out the questions they would like to ask each applicant. The applicants prepare the answers/statements for the questions they think will be asked.
	Step 3: The Borough Council group split into two groups, each interviewing two of the applicants (these are chosen by the group who prepared the interview) simultaneously while the other members of each applicant's group watch and listen.
	Step 4: The Borough Council group come together again and report on the interviews they have conducted. Then they decide which applicant to accept. Meanwhile the applicants talk about the interviews and give their impressions of what was said.
Remarks	In large classes there can be more applicants for the job.

118 Making a radio programme

Aims	*Skills* – all four skills
	Language – all elements
	Other – working on a task which produces a result that can be played to others
Level	Intermediate/advanced
Organisation	Class, groups, pairs
Preparation	Tape recorder and microphone, cassette recorder or record

player, sound effects record/cassette and music
record/cassette, collection of magazine/newspaper articles
with human interest stories, the use of more than one room

Time 3–5 hours

Procedure Step 1: Students may work on their own or in groups or
pairs. The end product should be a radio programme 10 to
20 minutes long, consisting of short interviews or
commentaries separated by advertising and music. Students
work on different parts of the programme and a schedule has
to be written up first of all with the different tasks clearly
specified.

Example:
Selecting and recording the music – 2 students
Presenters of the programme – 2 students
Sound effects – 2 students
First interview – 5 students
Second interview – 4 students
Advertisements – 6 students
Commentary – 3 students
Short sketch – 3 students
More items for the programme can be introduced with larger
classes.

Step 2: The students preparing the interviews and the
commentary look through the newspaper articles to find
suitable topics. When they have found a story they think
interesting they decide who to interview (e.g. in a case of
truancy they might want to record an interview with the
pupil concerned, his teacher and parents) and write up the
questions with the help of the teacher. The students working
out the advertisements look through the magazines to find
ideas they want to adapt. The teacher moves from group to
group to help and correct written material.

Step 3: Before the final recording each group presents its
part of the programme. Last minute alterations are made.
The presenters work out their introductory remarks to each
part of the programme. The sequence of the individual
interviews is fixed.

Step 4: Final recording.

Remarks A radio programme like this can be a valuable listening
exercise for other classes. It is surprising how many original
ideas the students will come up with once they get interested
in the project.

4.3 Stories

Activity	Topic type	Level	Organis- ation	Prep- aration	Time in minutes
119 Chain story	fict.	beg./int.	class	yes	10–20
120 Newspaper report	fact./fict.	int.	groups	yes	20–30
121 Picture stories	fact.	int.	pairs/indiv.	yes	15–20
122 Letters and telegrams	fact.	adv.	indiv.	Part 2	10–20
123 Keep talking	fact./pers.	int./adv.	indiv.	yes	5–15

pers. = personal; fact. = factual; beg. = beginners; int. = intermediate; adv. = advanced;
indiv. = individuals; groups = small groups; pairs = two people working together;
class = everybody working together; Part 2 = material for the exercise is to be found in Part 2.

The aim of these activities is to get the students to produce longer connected texts. For this they will need imagination as well as some skill in the foreign language. Stimuli are given in the form of individual words (No. 119 *Chain story*) or pictures (No. 120 *Newspaper report* and No. 121 *Picture stories*).

Story-telling activates more than a limited number of patterns and structures and these activities are best used as general revision. Similar exercises, in terms of their comprehensive scope, are No. 59 *Mad discussion* and No. 60 *Secret topic*, although these differ in their structure (dialogue).

119 Chain story

Aims	*Skills* – speaking
	Language – simple past
	Other – imagination, flexibility
Level	Beginners/intermediate
Organisation	Class
Preparation	Small slips of paper with one noun/verb/adjective on each of them, as many pieces of paper as there are students
Time	10–20 minutes
Procedure	*Step 1:* Each student receives a word slip.

Step 2: The teacher starts the story by giving the first sentence, e.g. 'It was a stormy night in November.' A student (either a volunteer or the person sitting nearest to the teacher) continues the story. He may say up to three sentences and must include the word on his slip of paper. The next student goes on.

Variations Each student is also given a number. The numbers determine the sequence in which the students have to contribute to the story.

Remarks One can direct the contents of the story to a certain degree by the choice of words.

120 Newspaper report

Aims *Skills* – writing
Language – reporting events, past tenses, passive
Other – imagination

Level Intermediate

Organisation Groups

Preparation A large number of photographs taken from magazines and newspapers

Time 20–30 minutes

Procedure *Step 1:* Each group is given five pictures of which they have to use three. Their aim is to write a newspaper report linking these three pictures.
Step 2: When each group has decided which pictures to use they write their report.
Step 3: The reports are read out and the pictures shown to the class.

Variations *1:* Each group chooses three pictures which another group has to write about.
2: After Step 2 all the pictures are displayed on the wall. When the reports are read out the others have to guess which pictures fit which report.
3: The reports are taken as starting points for interviews and role plays.

Remarks If unusual and widely differing pictures are chosen the result can be very funny.

121 Picture stories

Aims *Skills* – writing
Language – describing something, dialogue
Other – imagination

Level Intermediate

Organisation Pairs or individuals

Preparation	Pictures from magazines and cartoon strips with the words in the speech bubbles blanked out
Time	15–20 minutes
Procedure	The students have to write texts for the pictures or fill in the speech bubbles.
Variations	*1:* If more than one pair of students receive the same pictures/cartoon strips their results can be compared.
	2: One pair of students fills in the first speech bubble on a cartoon strip then hands the page to the next pair who fill in the next bubble, and so on. The first pair, in the meantime, fill in the first speech bubble on another strip, and then pass that on in the same way.

122 Letters and telegrams

Aims	*Skills* – writing, reading comprehension
	Language – nouns, verb forms
	Other – recognising unnecessary language
Level	Advanced
Organisation	Individuals
Preparation	A copy of the letter (Part 2) for each student
Time	10–20 minutes
Procedure	Each student receives a copy of a letter (see Part 2 for an example) and is asked to write two telegrams for it, one with 24 words, the other with 12 words. The telegrams are read out and compared.
Variations	Students receive different letters.

123 Keep talking

Aims	*Skills* – speaking
	Language – all elements
	Other – improvisation, flexibility, imagination
Level	Intermediate/advanced
Organisation	Individuals
Preparation	Slips of paper with both a sentence and a topic written on them
Time	5–15 minutes
Procedure	A student chooses a slip of paper and has to talk for one minute about the topic, beginning with the sentence on the piece of paper.

Examples:

Smoking	If a cigarette cost £1 a lot of people . . .
Homesickness	When I was a little boy/girl, . . .
Pets	I used to have . . ./I would like to have . . .
Parents	There are no certificates for good parents.
Clothes	I like . . .
Chewing gum	Animals don't chew chewing gum.

Variations   1: This can be played as a team contest.
    2: The topic and sentence cards can be prepared by the students.

Remarks   This activity can be used to revise topics that have been dealt with in class.

Solutions

No. 27   The same or different?
Same: 2,3,5,7,9,12,14,15,17
Different: 1,4,6,8,10,11,13,16,18

No. 28   Twins
Pictures which are identical: bottom right on 28A and third
down on the left on 28B.

No. 30   What are the differences?
Differences: left-hand pot plant on window sill, cat looking
in, birds in the sky, pencil flying through the air, coffee cup on
filing cabinet, label on filing cabinet, sheet of paper on desk of
black-haired typist, handbag of same typist, two pieces of
paper on filing cabinet in foreground, castors on chair.

No. 31   Ordering

A

7	1	11
4	9	3

B

5	6	
8	2	10

No. 51   NASA game
Oxygen, water, map, food, receiver/transmitter, rope, first
aid kit, parachute silk, life raft, signal flares, pistols, dried
milk, heating unit, magnetic compass, box of matches.

No. 103   Baker Street

12	14	16	18	20
Evans	Dudd	Charles	Birt	Abraham
married	spinster	bachelor	divorced	widower
tortoise rabbit	dog	canary	—	cat
thrillers	love stories	historical novels	Charles Dickens	TV
wine	beer	whisky	coffee	beer

Part 2

Worksheets

On the following pages, a broken line indicates where worksheets need to be cut up.

Identity cards

SURNAME

FIRST NAMES

Photo

ADDRESS

FAMILY

SCHOOL/UNIVERSITY   Main Subjects Studied

HOBBIES

OTHER INTERESTS

7

Stem sentences

Finish these sentences.

My favourite animals are ....

....

I like people who ....

....

I could not live without ....

....

I have never ....

If I had £100,000 I would ....

....

I am frightened of ....

....

.... make(s) me feel good.

Everybody should ....

....

The last time I laughed a lot was ....

....

I'd like to have ....

....

Groupings

Make hay	while the sun shines.
You can't teach	an old dog new tricks.
You scratch my back	and I'll scratch yours.
When the cat's away	the mice will play.
A new broom	sweeps clean.
A bad workman	always blames his tools.
All work and no play	makes Jack a dull boy.
Where there's a will	there's a way.
You may lead a horse to water	but you cannot make it drink.
If a thing is worth doing	it's worth doing well.
Don't put all your eggs	in one basket.
A bird in the hand	is worth two in the bush.

Summerhill was founded	in the year 1921.	My view is	that a child is innately wise and realistic.
Some children come to Summerhill	at the age of five years.	Children can go to lessons	or stay away from them.
The children generally remain at the school	until they are 16 years old.	In Summerhill	everyone has equal rights.
We generally have	about 25 boys and 20 girls.	All the same,	there is a lot of learning at Summerhill.
Only one or two older pupils	have rooms for themselves.	Hate breeds hate	and love breeds love.
No one tells them	what to wear.	Summerhill is possibly	the happiest school in the world.

139

Groupings

Groupings

– Would you like some coffee?	– What was the last film you saw?
– Yes, please.	– I can't remember. I never watch TV.
– With milk and sugar?	
– Just sugar. Two spoons, please.	– You should. There was a very good film on last night.
– What do you usually have for breakfast?	– Look at this. What could it be?
– I'm happy with anything, even soup.	– It looks like some kind of machine.
– Ugh! I couldn't eat soup for breakfast.	– Perhaps it's dangerous.
	– We'd better not touch it then.
– Two kilos of bananas, please.	– Excuse me, could you tell me the time, please?
– Would you like ripe ones or green ones?	– It's a quarter past four.
– Could you give me two ripe bananas and the rest green?	– Thank you.
– Excuse me, could you tell me the quickest way to the station, please?	– How long have you had your new bicycle?
– Sorry, I didn't catch what you said.	– About a year.
– What is the quickest way to the station, please?	– Are you happy with it?
– Catch a number 25 bus from the stop over there.	– Yes, very. It's light and fast.

Opinion poll

FOOD

Breakfast
You have to find out what the other people in your class usually have for breakfast.
Each of you prepares an interview card which could look like this:

Name	food?	drink?
Lisa	cornflakes	milk

FOOD

Drinks
You have to find out which drinks the people in your class like and dislike.
Each of you prepares an interview card which could look like this:

Name	likes?	dislikes?
Tina	milk, tea, water	orange juice

FOOD

Eating out
You have to find out whether the other people in your class ever eat out, and if so where they go.
Each of you prepares an interview card which could look like this:

Name	eats out?	where?
Tim	yes, sometimes	McDonald's

FOOD

Favourite meals
You have to find out the favourite meals (main course and dessert) of the other people in your class.
Each of you prepares an interview card which could look like this:

Name	favourite main course?	favourite dessert?
Chris	pizza	ice cream

FOOD

Food hates
You have to find out which meals or kinds of food the other people in your class dislike.
Each of you prepares an interview card which could look like this:

Name	food hates?
Freddie	chocolate, spinach

FOOD

Weight-watching
You have to find out if the other people in your class think they are too fat, just right or too thin.
Each of you prepares an interview card which could look like this:

	Do you think you are:		
Name	too fat?	just right?	too thin?
Bob	X		

FOOD

Cooking
You have to find out which meals or drinks the other people in your class can prepare themselves.
Each of you prepares an interview card which could look like this:

Name	can prepare/make?
Peter	tea, porridge, sandwiches, omelettes

Guided interviews

HOLIDAYS **A**

Ask your partner questions about his or her last holiday. Use the following notes to help you.

Where?
How long for?
Stay where?
With whom?
Like it? – Why? Why not?

Sightseeing?
Sports?
Food?
Go again?
Do anything special?

Bad points?

HOLIDAYS **B**

You can either answer your partner's questions by using the following notes or by talking about a holiday you really had.

Iceland
2 weeks
camping
group of students
very nice – nice people
   from different countries
a bit
hiking, swimming in lakes
a bit boring, no fruit
perhaps
climb a volcano, see a
   glacier
rain, cold

HOBBIES **A**

You can either answer your partner's questions by using the following notes or by talking about your real hobbies.

photography
surfing, playing chess
take photos on holiday,
   play chess with a friend
   once a week, surfing in
   summer
father plays chess, got
   camera as birthday present
surfing is fun, can play
   chess anywhere
film is expensive
need someone with a car
   for surf board

HOBBIES **B**

Ask your partner about his or her hobbies. Use the following notes to help you, but you can ask other questions as well.

What hobby?
Others?
How much time?
How started?
Why these?
Bad points?

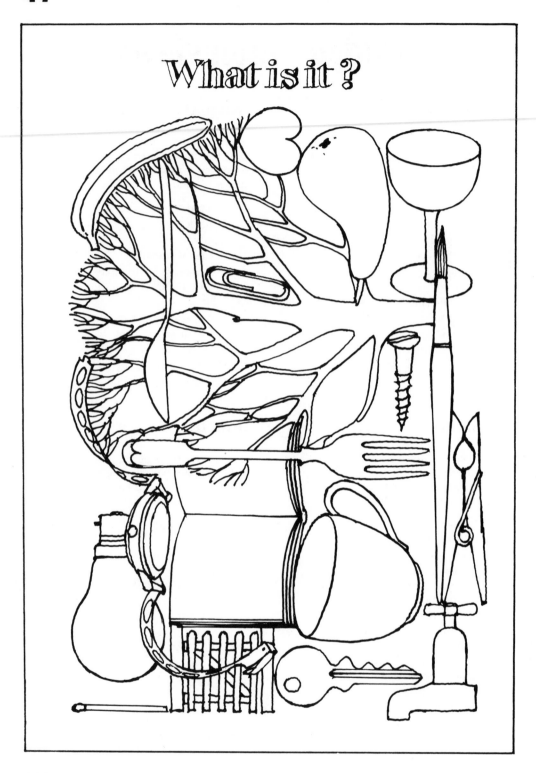

The same or Different?

A   B

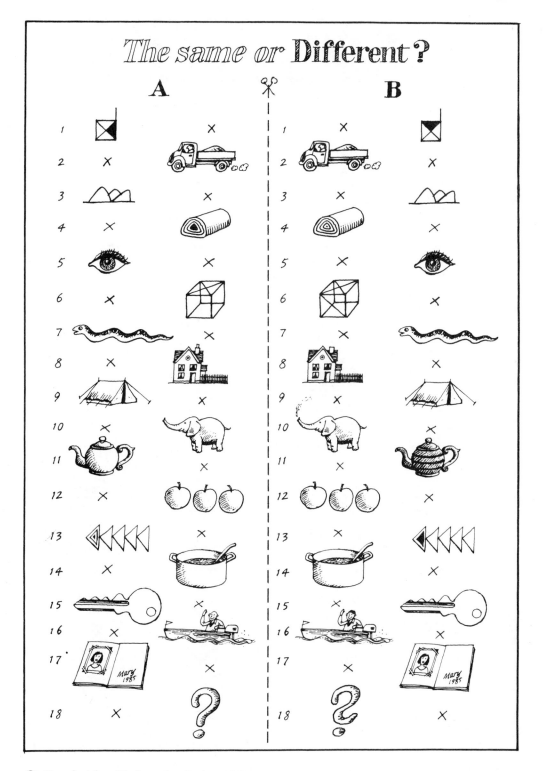

TWINS

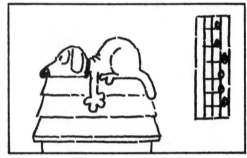

TWINS

Partner puzzle

What are the differences?

31
ORDERING

A

- ✂

B

TOWN PLAN

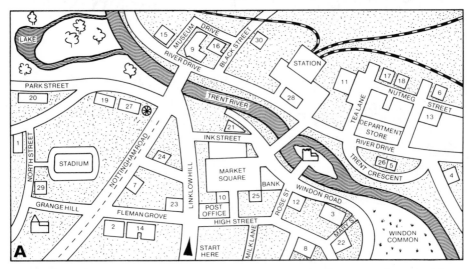

First find out all the names of the streets, parks and unnumbered buildings from your partner. Then write eight more names of places on the map (use the boxes numbered 1 to 15): a cinema, a supermarket, a school, an Indian restaurant, a library, a hospital, a pub, a bus station. Don't let your partner see what you have written, because he has to find these places. You have to find the following places, which your partner has written in: a Chinese restaurant, a police station, a bookshop, a petrol station, a kindergarten, a doctor's surgery, a hairdresser's, a swimming pool.

---✁------------------------------------

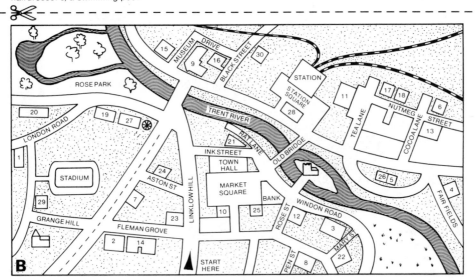

First find out all the names of the streets, parks and unnumbered buildings from your partner. Then write eight more names of places on the map (use the boxes numbered 16 to 30): a Chinese restaurant, a police station, a bookshop, a petrol station, a kindergarten, a doctor's surgery, a hairdresser's, a swimming pool. Don't let your partner see what you have written, because he has to find these places. You have to find the following places, which your partner has written in: a cinema, a supermarket, a school, a hospital, a pub, a bus station, an Indian restaurant, a library.

151

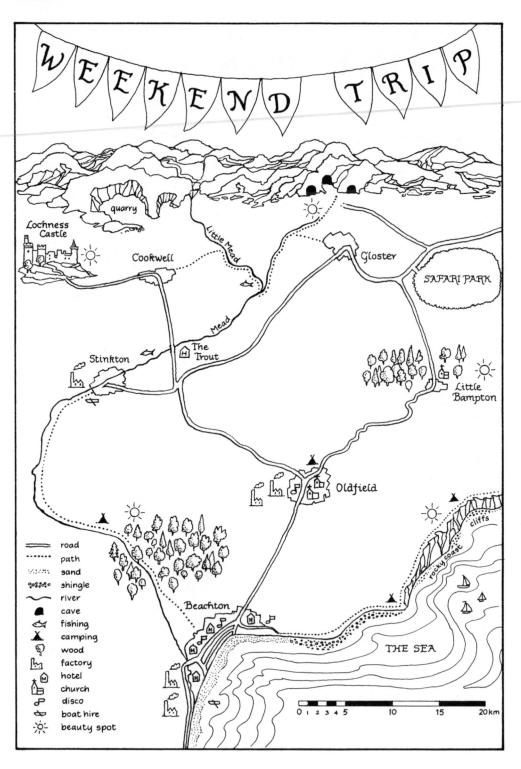

152   © Cambridge University Press 1984

WEEKEND TRIP

Information Card 1

– The sandy beaches near Beachton are polluted.

– There are dangerous currents off the rocky coast.

– 'The Trout' is a very nice country pub with good food but only a few rooms.

Information Card 2

– Little Bampton is a very picturesque village with a fine old church.

– There is a good market in Oldfield every Saturday where local crafts are sold.

– The caves are closed to the public on Sundays.

Information Card 3

– The famous Cookwell festival is being held at the weekend. There will be folk music, a fair, sheepdog trials and dancing.

– Bicycles can be hired at Oldfield.

– Tickets for the safari park cost £5.00.

Information Card 4

– Lochness Castle and Gardens are open to the public on Sundays from 10 a.m. to 4 p.m. (guided tours only).

– Beachton hotels are full at weekends. Rooms should be booked in advance.

– Oldfield has a museum with a lot of old farm machines, tools, clothes and furniture.

Information Card 5

– There is a sports day at Stinkton on Saturday. The sports fields, swimming pool, and equipment may be used free of charge.

– One can find interesting stones and fossils in the quarries near Cookwell.

– There is a special weekend ticket for all buses and trains for £5.00.

Information Card 6

– There is a very nice footpath from Cookwell along the Little Mead and the Mead to Gloster.

– The camping site near Oldfield is next to the main road and a petrol station.

– There are 'Bed and Breakfasts' in Cookwell, Gloster, Oldfield and Beachton.

35

Information search

(**For the teacher** The eight statements following the questions in the right-hand column are wrong. Plogs are scissors.)

Most plogs are made of metal.	**What are plogs?**
There are many kinds of plogs.	**What are plogs?**
You need plogs in the garden.	**What are plogs?**
In western countries there is at least one pair of plogs in every family.	**What are plogs?**
It is dangerous for children to use plogs.	**What are plogs?**
Most plogs have two holes.	Plogs are about one metre long.
You need plogs for sewing.	When you drop plogs onto the floor they break.
Surgeons, tailors and hairdressers need plogs.	Dogs use plogs.
Plogs can be opened and shut.	Plogs smell nice.
There are plogs for right-handed and left-handed people.	You can buy plogs at a baker's.
New plogs are sharp.	Plogs make good toys for young children.
Plogs have two parts which are screwed together.	Housewives never touch plogs.
You can hold plogs in one hand.	Plogs are not seen very often.
Ordinary plogs are about 20 centimetres long.	You can hurt people with plogs.
There are special plogs for beauty care.	Plogs are hard and pointed.
Most plogs have sharp points.	If you use plogs in the correct way on your hands it doesn't hurt.
Plogs do not burn.	You use plogs to make small pieces out of a big piece.
There are different plogs for all kinds of material: wire, cloth, paper.	Plogs are useful.

© Cambridge University Press 1984

JIGSAW

GUESSING

Group 1
Find these words:
1 You do it when you are tired.
2 You cannot .... milk or tea, but you
   can .... apples, bread, cake
   and chocolate.
3 You do it on horses and bicycles.
4 When two cars crash into
   each other, they have an ....
Make a word from the first letters of these
words.

The group word: A period of time.

Group 2
Find these words:
1 A big animal with grey skin and a trunk.
2 He delivers letters.
3 A kind of fruit, not an apple.
4 If you do not dislike something you .... it.
5 The time from noon till evening.
Make a word from the first letters of
these words.

The group word: A kind of fruit.

Group 3
Find these words:
1 Jingle Bells, Clementine and Old
   MacDonald are ....
2 You need a fork, a .... and a spoon for
   eating.
3 The first word in a letter.
4 Number between ten and twelve.
Make a word from the first letters of
these words.

The group word: A piece of furniture.

Group 4
Find these words:
1 Not young but ....
2 A hot drink, sometimes made from bags.
3 They were in North America before the
   Europeans came.
4 You are called by it.
Make a word from the first letters of
these words.

The group word: A preposition.

Group 5
Find these words:
1 When you ask a question you usually
   get an ....
2 In the sky at night, big and bright.
3 You write with it.
4 Last word in a letter to a good friend.
Make a word from the first letters of
these words.

The group word: It gives you light.

Group 6
Find these words:
1 A fruit and a colour.
2 Between two mountains.
3 If you have lots of money you are ....
4 Everything has a beginning and an ....
Make a word from the first letters of
these words.

The group word: A preposition.

Group 7
Find these words:
1 Something that is not easy is ....
2 Something that is not old is ....
3 Kangaroos and koalas live there.
4 If it was your birthday today people
   would say '.... birthday' to you.
Make a word from the first letters of
these words.

The group word: A part of the body.

Getting it together

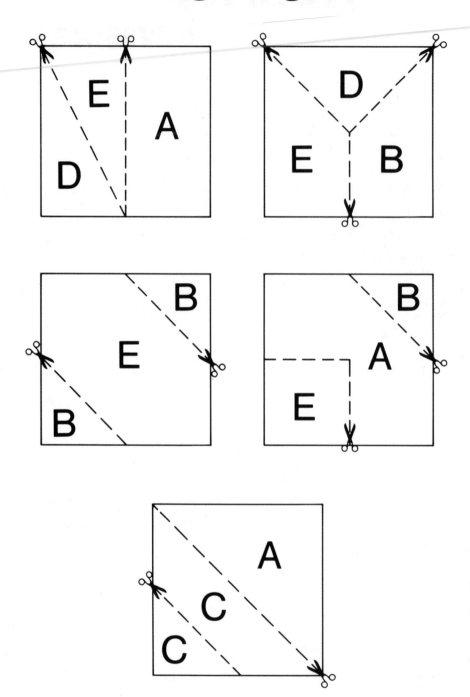

Question game

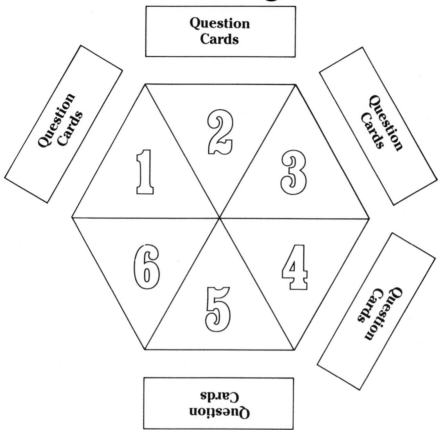

| Question Cards | | |

What kind of animal would you like to be? Why?	Where would you like to be right now? Why?	What gives you pleasure?
What would you give me as a birthday present?	If somebody gave you £50 what would you do with it?	What kind of weather do you like best?
What is the most important thing in the upbringing of children?	What would you like to achieve within the coming year?	
What would you like to change in your life?	Which human quality do you consider the most important?	

Go and find out

Find out who likes spiders, frogs and beetles.	Find out who can dance the tango.
Find out who has tea for breakfast.	Find out who has been on a walking holiday.
Find out who knows the capitals of Australia and New Zealand.	Find out who can cook a really good meal.
Find out who can knit.	Find out who reads a daily paper.
Find out who does not watch TV for more than two hours a week.	Find out who has more than one first name.
Find out who has been to London.	Find out who is able to use a washing-machine.
Find out who belongs to a club.	Find out who has more than 100 books.
Find out who usually sings in the bath.	Find out who knows what a *kiwi* is and where it lives.
Find out who works for a charity.	Find out who collects something unusual.
Find out who likes spinach.	Find out whose name has more than twenty letters.
Find out who likes to get up early.	Find out who likes horror films.
Find out who can sew on buttons and darn socks.	Find out who can repair a flat tyre on a bicycle.
Find out who likes classical music.	Find out who can play a musical instrument.
Find out who has an unusual hobby.	Find out who writes poems.
Find out who keeps a diary.	Find out who would like to be 10 years old again.
Find out who has had a holiday job.	Find out who can sing 'Auld Lang Syne'.

Find someone who...

chews chewing gum ....

likes doing jigsaw puzzles ....

likes to have very hot baths ....

reads more than one book a week ....

can tell you three meanings for [reɪn] ....

has been to Scotland ....

can tell you which language the word **cymru**
is taken from ....

can recite the alphabet in under 10 seconds ....

owns a pet with four legs ....

has got more than three brothers or sisters ....

is wearing something purple ....

has played this game before ....

pronounces these English towns correctly: Worcester, Gloucester,
Carlisle, Durham ....

has got a driving licence ....

likes liquorice ....

wears socks in bed ....

knows what **lads** and **lasses** are ....

can hum the tune of 'Yankee Doodle' ....

dreams about flying ....

collects something ....

believes in reincarnation ....

rolls their own cigarettes ....

can tell you a joke in English ....

likes working in the garden ....

has got a three-speed bicycle ....

was born on a Sunday ....

believes in ghosts ....

has flown in a helicopter or a glider ....

can speak another language apart from English and their
own language ....

goes jogging ....

Question and answer cards

A

Ask your partner questions
about Australia:
about its size
about its wildlife
about its native people

Big cities: Sydney, Melbourne,
Adelaide, Perth, Brisbane, Darwin

Flag:

Natural resources: uranium, coal,
iron ore, copper

B

Here are the answers to your partner's
questions:

Native people of Australia:
Aborigines – arrived 30,000 years
ago, many tribes, lived in harmony
with the land. Today: discrimination,
poverty.

Size: as big as Brazil

Wildlife: lots of animals not found
elsewhere, e.g. kangaroo, koala, emu.

Ask your partner questions
about Australia:
about the flag
about natural resources
about big cities

A

KEEPING FIT
Talk with your partner about
keeping fit.

Start like this:
1 What do you do about
    keeping fit?
2 ......
3 Would you like to do more
    or less?
4 ......
5 What do you think?
6 ......
Go on in this way.

B

KEEPING FIT
Talk with your partner about
keeping fit.

Answer his question then go on.
1 ......
2 What about you?
3 ......
4 Do you think it is important to
    keep fit? Why?
5 ......
6 ......?
Go on in this way.

© Cambridge University Press 1984

RANK ORDER

Read the questions and answers below carefully.
Rank all the answers to each question from 1 to 5. Give number 1 to the answer that applies to you most of all, number 2 to the second most applicable, and so on. Number 5 should always be the answer you least agree with.

1 Which would you least like to do tonight?
   □ go to the cinema and see a western
   □ listen to a Haydn symphony
   □ play Monopoly with friends
   □ mend clothes
   □ go to bed at 8p.m.

2 What would make you most uneasy?
   □ somebody praising you in front of others
   □ being in a large crowd
   □ meeting a new girlfriend's or boyfriend's parents for the first time
   □ people laughing at you
   □ seeing somebody cry

3 In which way do you learn best?
   □ by reading things out loud
   □ by having the radio on while you work
   □ by repetition
   □ by discussing things with someone else
   □ by making a lot of notes

4 Which would you most like to improve?
   □ your looks
   □ your attitude to work
   □ your social life
   □ your interest in current affairs
   □ your relations with your family

5 What would you like to take a course in?
   □ transcendental meditation
   □ basket weaving
   □ practical mathematics
   □ beauty care
   □ a foreign language

6 Which would you like to have a lot of money for?
   □ to travel a lot
   □ to be independent
   □ to buy things you like
   □ to spend freely on food and drink
   □ to help others in need

7 Which would you most like to have?
   □ one or two very close friends
   □ a large number of acquaintances
   □ five or six good friends
   □ just one friend
   □ both good friends and many acquaintances

8 Which is the quality your friends like most in you?
   □ your honesty
   □ your cheerfulness and good humour
   □ your reliability
   □ your willingness to listen and to help
   □ your generosity

GUIDE

Imagine that you have to work out a guided tour for a foreign delegation visiting your country. You want to show them places that you feel will give them a balanced impression of your people and country. Unfortunately the delegation will only be in your area for three days and you cannot show them everything. From the following list select ten places that the delegation should go and see and put them in order of importance.

a hospital
a home for mentally handicapped children
a coal mine
a nice pub
a nuclear power station
a cemetery
an art gallery
a botanical garden
some examples of modern architecture
a shopping precinct
a football stadium
a farm
a safari park
a poor housing area
a TV studio
a town hall
a secondary school
a historical museum
a medieval castle
a university
an airport
a water reservoir
a steel factory
a nature reserve

PRIORITIES

Why go to school?
Number these reasons in their order of importance from 1 (most important reason) to 12 (least important reason). Write the number in both boxes.

- -

☐ | ☐   to acquire general knowledge

☐ | ☐   to prepare for a job

☐ | ☐   to meet other young people

☐ | ☐   to train one's memory

☐ | ☐   to learn something about subjects one will not deal with again later

☐ | ☐   to find out what one is really interested in

☐ | ☐   to give one's parents some peace and quiet

☐ | ☐   to test one's intelligence

☐ | ☐   to learn how to study and work with books

☐ | ☐   to have a good time

☐ | ☐   to be kept dependent

☐ | ☐   to learn discipline and order

Check

You are one of the crew on board a spaceship to rendezvous with the mother ship on the lighted side of the moon. Mechanical difficulties, however, have forced your ship to crash-land at a spot some 300 kilometres from the rendezvous point. The rough landing has damaged much of the equipment aboard. Your survival depends on reaching the mother ship, and you have to choose the most essential items for the 300 km. trip. The 15 items left intact after landing are listed below. Your task is to rank them in order of their importance to your crew in your attempt to reach the rendezvous point. Write number 1 for the most important item, number 2 for the second most important item, and so on through to number 15.

box of matches

concentrated food

20 metres of nylon rope

parachute silk

portable heating unit

two .45 calibre pistols

one case of tins of dried milk

two 50 kilo tanks of oxygen

star map

life raft

magnetic compass

20 litres of water

signal flares

first-aid kit

solar-powered FM receiver/transmitter

LOOKING
for a job

WANTED
experienced
SOCIAL WORKER

Preferably full-time, to work in Fairview Estate. Needs car. Some evening and weekend work. Council flat available. Salary £7,000 p.a.

Apply to Lindon Borough Council, P.O. Box 106, Lindon.

Fairview Council Estate

built 1968-72, many high-rise flats; high incidence of truancy and juvenile delinquency, large number of one-parent families; no youth club; widespread vandalism; large proportion of old-age pensioners; one pub; secondary modern school, two primary schools.

APPLICANTS

Freda Hastings, 35
Divorced; 2 children aged 8 and 6; trained as a social worker 10 years ago; no employment in the last eight years; no car; would like half-time job; cannot work evenings or weekends; bad health; cheerful personality; likes children; needs a bigger flat.

Harold Winter, 23
Single; just finished training as a social worker; some experience in running a youth club; has a motor-bike; not many friends; spends more than he earns; insecure personality; likes working evenings; wants £7,200 p.a.

Sue and Mike Darrell, 28 and 32
Married; 3 children aged 6, 4 and 1; both trained social workers; went to work in Africa for six years after training; would like to share the job because of the children; will not accept any job for less than £4,000 each p.a.; no car; would like a house; very interested in political work; no experience in working with old people; do not want to work weekends.

Robert Ludlow, 49
Married; no children; has a car; worked as lorry driver, barman and night watchman before training as a social worker 10 years ago; has had five jobs in the last four years; suffered from alcoholism, now cured after therapy; marriage problems; a bit short-tempered; wants to make a new start; gets on well with older people; very strict with children and youngsters.

56

GOOD TEACHER

A good teacher

◯ keeps in contact with the parents of his or her pupils and lets them participate in the life of the school (in a primary or secondary school)

◯ is able to maintain discipline and order

◯ lets the students share his or her own life with all its ups and downs

◯ works hard to remain up-to-date in his or her subject

◯ openly admits when he or she has made a mistake or does not know something

◯ is interested in his or her students, asks them about their homes and tries to help where possible

◯ makes the students work hard and sets high standards

◯ is friendly and helpful to his or her colleagues

◯ uses a lot of different materials, equipment and teaching methods and attempts to make his or her lessons interesting

◯ helps the students become independent and organise their own learning

Shrinking story

THE BEAR SAYS NORTH

(Finnish Folk Tale)

ONE DAY, while Osmo the Bear was prowling about the forest, he caught a grouse.

"Pretty good," he thought to himself. "Won't the other animals be surprised when they hear old Osmo has caught a grouse?"

He was very proud of his feat and he wanted all the world to know of it. So, holding the grouse carefully in his teeth without hurting it, he began parading it up and down the forest paths.

"They'll certainly envy me this nice plump grouse," he thought. "They won't be so ready to call me awkward and lumbering after this!"

Presently Mikko the Fox sauntered by. He at once saw that Osmo was showing off, and he made up his mind the Bear should not get the admiration he wanted. So he pretended not to see the grouse at all. Instead he pointed his nose upward and sniffed.

"Um! um!" grunted Osmo, trying to attract attention to himself.

"Ah," said Mikko in an offhand way, "is that you, Osmo? Which way is the wind blowing to-day? Can you tell me?"

Osmo could not, of course, answer without opening his mouth, so he grunted, hoping Mikko would see the grouse, and understand why he couldn't speak. But the Fox didn't glance at him at all. With his nose still pointing upward, he kept sniffing the air.

"It seems to be from the south," said he. "It is from the south, isn't it Osmo?"

"Um! um!" repeated Osmo, growing more impatient every moment.

"Not from the south, you say? Then which way is it blowing?"

By this time the Bear was so cross with Mikko, he forgot all about his grouse, he just opened his mouth, and roared out, "North!"

Of course the moment he opened his mouth the grouse flew away.

"Now, see what you've done!" he stormed angrily. "You've made me lose my nice plump grouse!"

"I?" said Mikko. "What had I to do with it?"

"You kept asking me about the wind until I opened my mouth – that's what you did!"

The Fox shrugged his shoulders.

"Why did you open your mouth then?"

"Well, you can't say 'north' without opening your mouth, can you?" the Bear demanded.

The Fox laughed and laughed.

"See here, Osmo, don't blame me. Blame yourself. If I'd had the grouse in my mouth and you'd asked me about the wind, I'd never have said 'north'!"

"What would you have said?" asked the Bear.

Mikko, the rascal, laughed harder than ever. Then he clenched his teeth together and said "EAST"!

FUTURES

	Today	Next week	Next year	My lifetime	My children's lifetime
The world					
My country					
My locality					
My place of work/ study					
My family					
Myself					

Here and Now →

TIME ⟶

	Today	Next week	Next year	My lifetime	My children's lifetime
The world					
My country					
My locality					
My place of work/ study					
My family					
Myself					

Here and Now →

TIME ⟶

What evidence?

There are fifteen tables in this room.

Maud will never be able to sing in tune.

Peter is conservative.

Men are better cooks than women.

Children like ice cream.

There are a hundred centimetres in one metre.

Rachel is intelligent.

Hiroshima was destroyed in 1945.

Violence on TV makes people more aggressive.

Spiders have eight legs.

A car is more expensive than a bicycle.

Pop music is horrible.

Life is hard.

Girls are better storytellers than boys.

Cacti grow better in sunlight than in the shade.

Discussion

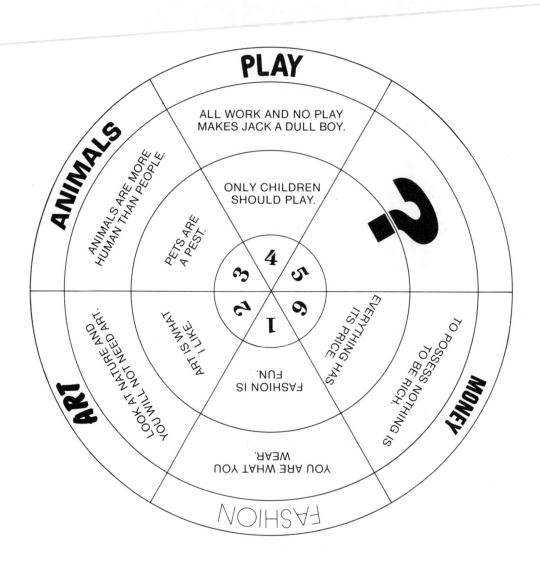

Wheel

Aims in life

NEXT YEAR

areas

⬭	
⬭	
⬭	
⬭	
⬭	

- travel
- job
- family
- friends
- hobby
- partner

NEXT 5 YEARS

⬭	
⬭	
⬭	
⬭	

- possessions
- appearance
- qualifications
- learning

NEXT 30 YEARS

⬭	
⬭	
⬭	

- lifestyle
- the world

Values continuum

	Agree strongly	Agree somewhat	Neither agree nor disagree	Disagree somewhat	Disagree strongly
Beating children is sometimes necessary.					
People who tell lies steal as well.					
For every problem there is only one correct solution.					
Where there's a will there's a way.					
Think before you act.					
Proverbs are usually true.					
We can learn a lot from the past.					
Modern problems cannot be solved by old methods.					
People can be changed by education.					
Never fight against things you cannot change by yourself.					
It's never too late.					
Everybody is different.					

Miracle workers

A group of 15 experts are offering their services. Success is guaranteed for their methods.

1 *Claire Voyant*

Everything you want to know about the future will be answered by her and she will train you to become a clairvoyant as well.

2 *Jack Goldrich*

He will help you to become an expert at making money. You will never be poor again.

3 *Dr B. U. Tiful*

She is an expert in cosmetic surgery and will help you to achieve the appearance you have always dreamed of. She can even alter your height and shape.

4 *Prof. I. Q. Clever*

He will help you become very intelligent.

5 *Robinson Crusoe*

He is a specialist in adventures and exciting trips to foreign countries. Your life will be dangerous but never boring.

6 *A. L. L. Wright*

Learn how to be optimistic. Even in the most depressing situation you will always see a good point.

7 *B. Oldcastle*

She is the expert on growing old. You will learn how to accept old age and lead an interesting and fulfilling life after 60.

8 *Alex Fame*

He will help you to become famous. Whatever you do you will be well-known everywhere.

9 *Art Iste*

Develop your artistic abilities. Art Iste will help you become a good painter or sculptor, a photographer or a draughtsman. Your art will be talked about and bought by the world's leading museums.

10 *Pop Ular*

He will make you popular with lots of people. You will always have a lot of friends.

11 *M. O. Ther*

She will help you with your family life. It will be very happy and satisfying.

12 *St Valentine*

He is an expert on love. With his help you will find the right partner.

13 *I. N. Sight*

She will give you self-knowledge and insight into your own personality.

14 *O. K. Work*

He will help you find the job which is right for you.

15 *I. Dear*

She is an expert on originality. She will help you become full of ideas for every situation in your life and your job as well as your hobbies and family life.

Unfinished sentences

The funniest thing I ever saw was ....

If I had 24 hours to live ....

On Saturdays I usually ....

I feel best when people ....

I'd like to spend a long holiday in ....

I wish politicians would ....

I have never ....

Parents should always ....

My children will ....

This world would be a better place if ....

The thing that worries me most is ....

I never worry about ....

Some day I am going to ....

I like people who ....

I get very angry if ....

I find it difficult to ....

I'd like to be more .... and less ....

I am not interested in ....

Studying is ....

If I could be somewhere else now, I'd ....

© Cambridge University Press 1984

VALUES TOPICS

START HERE

happiness	a country you are interested in	the season you like best	a nice present you were given	QUESTION / FREE	what you do in the evenings	fun	a good friend

a frightening experience

FREE / QUESTION

something you are proud of

your favourite subject at school

your last holiday

your family

something dangerous

FREE / QUESTION

your plans for next week

a TV programme you like

FREE / QUESTION

something you lost recently

a game you like playing

how you get to school/work

your room

what you did last Sunday

FREE / QUESTION

your favourite kind of music

something you are good at

your taste in clothes

FREE / QUESTION

a good book you have read

something you like doing

your pet

QUESTION / FREE

animals

what makes you laugh

something you worry about

FREE / QUESTION

a dream you had

your hopes for the future

a job you would like

something you would like to possess

your feelings about smoking

your ideas about the ideal wife or husband

your happiest moment in the last year

your ideal flat/house

something you do not like doing

FREE / QUESTION

something you think is stupid

your most important possession

your feelings about this game

QUESTION / FREE

an adventure

a lucky day

START AGAIN?

TELL US ABOUT

Viewpoints

Mary Taylor, 35, housewife (physics and maths teacher) would like to go back to teaching, feels unfulfilled at home, has an offer of a job in a nearby school; a friend of hers is a teacher there.

Mark Taylor, 40, architect, is understanding, does not mind Mary working, has a demanding job, no time or desire to help in the house, feels that Mary might have forgotten a lot about her subjects.

Moira Taylor, 8, at school, is afraid her mother will have less time for her when working; would like a brother or sister.

Margaret Taylor, 68, widow, Mark's mother, runs a bookshop, has been working all her life, supports Mary, lives far away.

Frank and Elizabeth Martin, 70 and 58, Mary's parents, retired postman and housewife, both very much against Mary going back to work, feel both Moira and Mark would suffer, think Mary has everything she needs, live in the next street, come and see their daughter very often.

Gordon Parsons, 45, headmaster of the school, thinks women cannot be good mathematicians, but thinks women are good at classroom management, desperately needs a physics and maths teacher for his school, feels that Mary is a bit shy and may not know about the latest developments in her subjects.

Desperate Decision

You are Susan Munden, a 35 year-old teacher on a hiking trip in the Scottish Highlands with a group of seven pupils, three boys and four girls aged between 13 and 16. You are carrying your own food and tents. You have planned to be out of contact with other people for a whole week and are expected on Sunday at a small village on the Scottish west coast where you will be picked up by a bus.

Today is Thursday. It has been raining steadily since Tuesday night and everyone is wet and cold. You know that you have not come as far as you should have done by this time, and you start feeling anxious about getting to the meeting point on Sunday. During the morning a dense fog starts coming down, and within half an hour the mountains and the path are covered in thick fog. You have to walk by compass now, which slows the group down even further.

At lunchtime two boys and two girls start complaining about stomach pains, diarrhoea and feeling sick. You suspect that some of the water you took from mountain streams may have been contaminated. In the afternoon they feel worse and can only walk very slowly. While climbing down a steep hillside the youngest girl, Rosie, stumbles and falls. She cannot get up. Her leg is broken. You set up camp and discuss with your group what is to be done.

You are in a valley between two mountain ridges. The nearest road is about 15 kilometres away as the crow flies, but there is no path across the mountains and the moor is beyond them. There is no bridge across the river, and with all the rain of the last few days it may be too deep to wade across.

About 5 kilometres back the way you have come, a relatively easy path turns off which takes you to a lake and a fisherman's hut about 30 kilometres away. However, you do not know whether anybody lives in the hut or whether it has a phone. The next village is about 40 kilometres away. About 10 kilometres back the way you have come there is a small forest where you could find some firewood. You have enough food till Sunday and there are mountain streams nearby. You also have camping gas cookers and enough gas for three hot drinks and two warm meals a day, but there is no firewood. The only people who can read a map and use a compass, apart from you, are one of the sick boys and Fiona, the oldest girl (she is feeling all right). Rosie is in a lot of pain and needs a doctor soon.

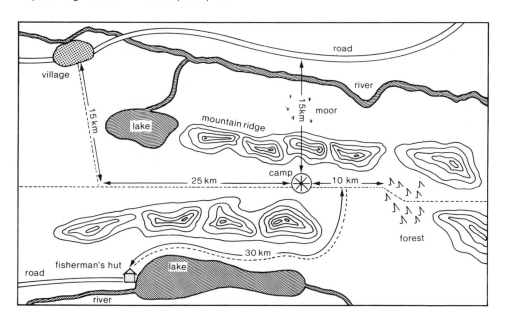

What can you do?
Think of all the possible courses of action and decide on the best one. Give reasons for your choice.

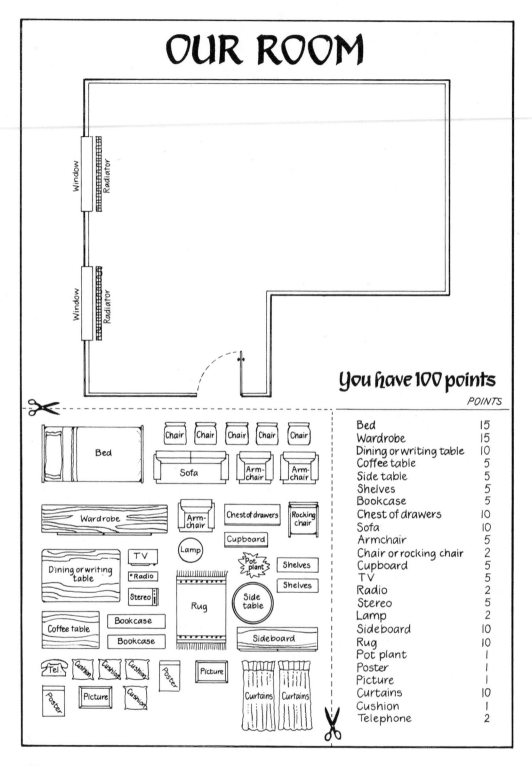

GROUP HOLIDAY

HELP ON FARM ON SMALL GREEK ISLAND

FOOD AND ACCOMMODATION FREE

WORK 6 DAYS A WEEK PLUS FREE EXTRA WEEK

Be Your Own **CAPTAIN**

Comfortable Boat
(Sleeps 6-8)
For a Cruise Down the Shannon

See the Cultural and Historic parts of Europe Italy and France by Coach

London
Paris
Lyon
Arles Cannes Venice
Florence
Rome
Naples

SMALL HOTELS BED & BREAKFAST

RELAX

FINNISH LAKE
Swim, Fish, Sauna, Canoe
Stay in Wooden Hut
Provide Own Meals

TWO WEEKS IN MALLORCA

FIRST CLASS HOTEL (ALL INCL)
Disco · Bar · Trips · Entertainment · Good Food

Like Robinson Crusoe

CRUISE ON SMALL STEAMER IN THE ADRIATIC

PROVIDE OWN FOOD

RAIL ROVER TICKET
EUROPE FOR TWO WEEKS
AND YOUTH HOSTEL VOUCHERS

YOUR SUGGESTION?

HIKE ALONG THE PENNINES

CAMPING + GOOD HOTELS
ALL FOOD, MAPS AND
GUIDE INCLUDED

*AT THE END
A WEEKEND IN THE LAKE DISTRICT*

Friendly Biscuits Inc.

You know that: *Ron Preedy* is on the board of directors, he has an all-female staff.

A   *Philippa Gordon* is personal assistant to one of the other directors.

John Martin is the only male secretary, but he does not work together with the male typist.

You know that: There are three directors, a personal assistant, secretary and typist for each director.

B   All in all there are four men and eight women.

The personal assistants are *Mary Hill, Angela Woodhouse* and *Philippa Gordon*.

You know that: Only one of the typists and one of the secretaries is a man.

C   The male secretary works for *Angela Woodhouse*, who is assistant to *Brenda Pilot*.

Sheila Rogers is not *Philippa Gordon's* typist.

You know that: *Christina Stead* is the only typist working for a male secretary.

D   Director *David Parsons* is quite content both with *Roger Haldane* as typist and *Jean Carter* as secretary.

Carole Ward would rather work for *Angela Woodhouse*. Her typist *Sheila Rogers* cannot understand that.

BAKER STREET

Miss Dudd owns a dog.

✂ ┈┈┈┈┈┈┈┈┈┈┈┈┈┈┈┈┈┈┈┈┈┈┈┈┈┈┈┈┈┈┈┈┈┈

The woman at No. 12 has two pets; a tortoise and a rabbit.

The dog owner drinks beer.

Mrs Evans is married.

Mr Abraham is a widower; his neighbour is divorced.

The married woman reads thrillers.

The woman who likes coffee does not own a pet.

No. 18 is the only house without a pet.

There are five pets in Baker Street; a cat, a dog, a canary, a rabbit and a tortoise.

The bachelor likes historical novels.

Mr Abraham cannot read, he watches TV.

The widower and the spinster like beer.

Mrs Birt likes to read books by Charles Dickens.

The whisky drinker owns a canary.

The dog owner living next door to the bachelor is keen on love stories.

Mr Charles lives between Miss Dudd and Mrs Birt.

The married woman drinks wine.

The pet at No. 14 is a dog.

Mr Abraham lives at No. 20.

The dog owner and the cat owner do not live next to each other.

104A

Problem Page (1)

Will marriage bring love? ➊

Dear Mary,

I recently broke up with a man I loved and he married another girl.

I have been going out with someone else ever since. He's 29 and I'm 26.

Now he has asked me to marry him and I suppose I would be mad to refuse.

But I don't love him, though I'm fond of him. I live in a small village so I'm unlikely to get another chance. I don't want to be left on the shelf.

My mother says love grows if you marry someone who is good to you. Do you think she's right?

Miss P. J., Suffolk

I'm restless ➋

Dear Mary,

Six years ago, when I was 24, I married my first and only boyfriend.

We now have two lovely children and my husband is good and kind. I should be happy, but I'm not.

I feel that life is passing me by and that I married too young. And I am now building a fantasy world around a friend's husband. I suppose I should be ashamed. Can you help me?

(Mrs R. McC.)

Dear Mary, ➌

I have been seeing a young man once or twice a week for the past year. I enjoy his company and have always regarded him as a good friend.

He has been very good to me and bought me anything I have asked for. But lately he has talked of marriage. He seems to assume that I am serious about him and will eventually settle down in some dull little semi in the suburbs.

But I have no intention of even contemplating marriage for years yet. And he isn't successful enough or rich enough to be the man I would choose.

I don't want to hurt him or frighten him off because he does give me a good time. But how can I get over to him that I am only prepared to allow him to be in my company, and not my future husband.

(Miss R.W.)

Dear Mary, ➍

I have been living with my boyfriend for two years. I am now pregnant and having a dreadful time with my family because they are trying to pressure us into getting married.

I cannot accept their reasoning that it would be for the good of the child.

By the time the baby is of school age, marriage will be a thing of the past anyway. When will people accept a more liberal outlook on life?

(Ms K. O'M.)

Two-timer ➎

Dear Mary,

We work in the typing pool of a large London store and are very concerned for the welfare of one of our young colleagues.

She is only 19, unmarried, and has become very friendly with a young man who works in one of the departments of the store. He pops into the typing pool to see her and they hold hands, whisper, and act as if we are not there. We know that he is engaged to a girl who lives near him.

We feel for the protection of the girl, that we should complain to the general manager. But we wouldn't like anybody to get the sack.

(Four Worried Typists)

I don't want to be alone ➏

Dear Mary,

I have been married for just over a year. We were lucky enough to buy a house, although we had to move away from both our families. It is very nice, but we have made very few friends. Now my husband's job is taking him up North for six weeks and I can't bear the thought of being on my own.

(Mrs T. E.)

Problem Page (1)

1

I think she could be right but I wouldn't take any bets on it. And I certainly wouldn't bet on the success of a marriage that's based on the fear of never getting another chance.

It's pretty insulting to marry a man just because you're afraid no one else will ask you.

Imagine how you'd feel if the position was reversed – and he was willing to wed you as a last resort. Wouldn't you resent it?

Maybe you think he'll never realise the reason you accepted him, but he's bound to get the message, for no one can keep up a pretence of love for long.

You'd be far better off unwed than married to a man who might bore you or irritate you or even repel you.

Passionate love can overcome the minor irritations and often even the major ones.

Where there's no love, there really isn't much hope either.

Why don't you show a little enterprise and get out of your village? There's a big world waiting outside.

2

It sounds to me as if you need a new interest, and I don't mean another man. Everybody starts feeling restless now and again. But provided you are sensible it will pass.

3

I suppose it is difficult to tell a man who obviously loves you that all you want from him is what you can grab. You are not a fool and you know that sooner or later you are going to hurt him badly.

Be straightforward with him now. Think of him for once rather than of yourself and what you might be missing out on if he never saw you again.

4

You may be right about marriage being a thing of the past in a few years, but I wouldn't bet on it. Of course, you are entitled to live as you think fit. But I hope that when your child is old enough to think for himself, he agrees with your point of view. If he doesn't, then you are going to face a heap of problems.

5

My advice is simple – mind your own business. The girl is old enough to know what she is doing.

6

Why not find yourself a job to keep you occupied? You can keep in touch with him by telephone. If it's important to his job that he should work away from home for a few weeks, don't let him know the parting will upset you.

183

Problem page (2)

LETTERS

So shy

This girl has lived in our neighbourhood for five years, but though she fascinates me I have never plucked up enough courage to speak to her.

I'm also interested in a girl I see at work, and another one I meet at the bus stop. In fact there are lots of attractive girls in my vicinity. Why haven't I enough nerve to approach them?

Hesitating

Holiday romance

Earlier this year I went with my parents to Majorca for a holiday. I was very fed up at the time and I met and fell in love with a waiter from another hotel. It's really love and it's changed my whole life. The trouble is that now I'm back home just writing to Pepe isn't enough. I want to go back to him, but I can't on my own as I'm 16, and on my dad's passport. Please don't think it's infatuation 'cos it's not. Pepe feels the same. We're both Catholic.

Mary (Liverpool)

ANSWERS

Dear Hesitating,

You don't sound as if you have enough nerve to approach a puff of thistledown and that's what must be in your brain-box if you're content to carry on this way.

I suggest you peer in the mirror, open your mouth and look closely at the little pink object behind your lips. It's called your tongue. Until you start using it you'll never get a girlfriend.

Dear Mary,

If you really love Pepe, Mary, it won't matter if you have to wait a while before you are able to go back to him. I suggest you discuss the whole matter with your parents and then perhaps you could arrange with Pepe that he comes over and visits you and your family this summer so that you can really get to know each other again.

© Cambridge University Press 1984

Telephoning

You are Robin

A You are in a hurry because you are going out in half an hour and want to wash and dry your hair beforehand. Your phone rings.

You are Francis/Frances

B You and your boy or girlfriend have just split up and you desperately need someone to talk to. You ring up your friend Robin.

You are Gene/Jean

A You are studying for an important exam next week and are just struggling with a difficult book. When you think that you have just worked out what one chapter means the phone rings. You know you have to go back to your book quickly so as not to forget what you worked out.

You are Nick/Nicky

B You have just come home from the most fantastic weekend trip you have ever had. You went to a log cabin on a lonely lake with some other students. There you did your own cooking, lots of sports and had a party every night. You are really eager to tell your friend all about it so you ring her or him up.

You are Ricky

A You are in the kitchen baking a cake as a surprise for your parents. Your parents will be home in two hours. The phone rings.

You are Mrs Fletcher

B You are 75 years old and have sprained your ankle. It is very difficult for you to walk. You need someone to do some shopping for you. And you really would like to tell the young man or girl who lives on the top floor in your building all about your fall. You ring him or her up.

Controversy in the school

Dear Principal,

As part of our work in Modern Studies Renato Romo has been invited to come and talk to us tomorrow. He is an actor who is in a play at the Globe Theatre this week. He is a refugee from Chile, where he was tortured. Would you like us to bring him to meet you? If so could you suggest a time?

R. Barnett, G. Wright (Form 4 G)

Letting Us Down

We have said it before. Alas, we have to say it again. This country is going from bad to worse. The crime rate is soaring. Television is daily more shocking. Freedom is being worn away. The government is not respected. We have lost our influence in the world.

The trouble has many causes. But one cause is definitely our schools. Our schools are letting us down. The lack of discipline. The free and easy methods. Worst of all, the time spent on 'Modern Studies', or whatever the latest jargon is.

But it is very important indeed that children should be made to learn the traditional school subjects. And they should be made to learn about the past. Particularly the past of this great country. Only then will they have the courage to face the present.

Dear Principal,

My child is in Form 4G, where they are doing some work called Modern Studies. I am rather worried about this. Surely the most important thing at school is to learn to pass exams, in order to get a good job in later life. But the pupils are not really learning anything useful in this Modern Studies work. I do not think it is going to help them pass their exams, and it seems to do nothing but confuse them. Can you reassure me?

Yours sincerely,

MEMO

from: Deputy Principal

to: Principal

re: Local press/modern studies

I enclose a cutting from today's local paper. Perhaps you have seen it? Sounds as if it's a direct reference to some of the Modern Studies work at this school. Ought we to reply? My own view is that indeed M.S. has little or no value, and is a cause of bad behaviour and lower standards. Is this a chance to put a brake on it, or stop it altogether?

Dear Principal,

Our work in Modern Studies is going very well. The students are getting a lot out of it. Some of them are keen to make two visits - one to a 'factory farm' about 20 kilometres away, to see how valuable protein from third world countries is being used to fatten up cows and pigs. And the other to an experimental commune about 50 kilometres away which specialises in organic farming and low-impact technology. Could you please let me know whether funds are available for these two visits?

Yours, B. Warren.

LETTERS
& TELEGRAMS

Dear Mum and Dad,

    I tried to ring you earlier today, but couldn't get through for some reason. Now I've borrowed some notepaper and stamps just to let you know what has happened. Last night in the Youth Hostel at Innsbruck someone stole my money, my passport, my interrail card and my camera. I'm furious that I hadn't put everything in my sleeping-bag with me as I usually do. This morning I went straight to the police, but they weren't very hopeful about getting my things back. The thief has probably cleared out of the country.

    I've hitch-hiked to Salzburg to try and get some help from Uncle Harry and Auntie May but they seem to be away. All the blinds are down and nobody answers the phone. Still, they aren't expecting me till next week. I don't know where or how I'll sleep tonight. Perhaps at the station. Thank god it's warm.

    Please, please, could you send some money as quickly as possible care of the Main Post Office !! I wish I had the money for a telegram! Do hurry. I'll try to do something about the passport and interrail card tomorrow. But money is the most important thing. I've got very little food left.

        Love
        Mike

Alphabetical table of activities

Activity	No.	Page	Materials	Organisation	Time	Aims/tasks
A day in the life	18	33	none	groups	15–20	inventing and guessing a daily programme
Adverb charade	106	116	paper	pairs, class	10–15	miming and guessing actions
Ageless	44	56	questions	groups	10–20	discussing one's attitude to various ages
Aims in life	78	90	Part 2	individuals, groups	15–20	describing and giving reasons for one's aims in life
Alternatives	90	99	situations	class	5–20	listing possible actions and discussing them
Awards	73	85	none	class, groups	25–45	creating awards and discussing candidates for them
Back to back	11	22	music	pairs	10–20	describing appearance and clothing
Baker Street	103	112	Part 2	class	5–15	cooperating in solving a puzzle
Brainstorming	87	96	none	groups	5–15	finding as many ideas as possible
Chain story	119	130	word cards	class	10–20	telling a story
Choosing pictures	8	19	pictures	individuals	15–20	giving reasons for the selection of a certain picture
Clusters	9	19	music, commands	class	15–30	understanding instructions
Coffeepotting	22	35	room	groups	10–15	guessing activities
Comments	66	81	none	class	15–20	writing comments on people and discussing them
Consequences	89	98	situations	groups, class	10–20	listing and discussing consequences
Controversy in the school	114	125	Part 2	groups, class	20–45	preparing a role play in groups
Daily life	108	117	dialogues	groups	15–20	acting out dialogues, guessing
Definitions	24	37	dictionary	class, teams	10–20	inventing definitions and guessing
Desert island (1)	50	63	list	pairs, class	10–20	choosing objects and giving reasons for their selection
Desert island (2)	92	103	none	individuals, pairs, groups	10–20	listing objects necessary for survival
Desperate decision	94	104	Part 2	groups	30–40	finding solutions to a problem
Discussion wheel	74	86	Part 2, dice	groups	15–25	discussing various topics
Everyday problems	101	111	none	groups, class	10–15	sharing personal problems

Activity	No.	Page	Materials	Organisation	Time	Aims/tasks
Find someone who . . .	42	54	Part 2	individuals, class	10–20	questioning the other group members
Fire	95	105	none	individuals	5–10	listing objects and defending one's choice
Four corners	75	86	notices, room	class, groups	20–30	comparing preferences
Friendly Biscuits Inc.	102	111	Part 2	groups	10–20	cooperating in solving a puzzle
Futures	65	80	Part 2	individuals, groups	20–30	filling in a table and discussing it
Getting it together	38	49	Part 2	groups	20–45	cooperation in a task and discussing the shared experience
Go and find out	41	54	Part 2	individuals, class	15–30	finding out things by questioning others
Good teacher	56	70	Part 2	individuals	15–20	ranking qualities
Group holiday	100	110	Part 2	groups	15–20	agreeing on a shared holiday
Groupings	10	20	Part 2	class, groups	5–10	matching words, proverbs, etc.
Group interview	14	26	none	groups	5–15	asking and answering questions
Guarantees	55	68	list	teams	30–40	giving sales talks
Guide	48	61	Part 2	groups	15–30	ranking places for a sightseeing tour
Guided interviews	16	29	Part 2	pairs, groups	15–25	interviewing each other
Hidden sentence	26	38	sentence cards	teams, individuals	20–30	guiding the conversation
Hotel receptionist	109	118	messages	class, groups	15–20	miming a request
Ideal day	85	95	none	individuals	20–30	describing an ideal day
Identity cards	4	16	Part 2	pairs	10–30	interviewing and introducing a partner
I'd rather be . . .	84	94	word list	class	5–15	giving associations
Information search	35	47	Part 2	groups	10–15	putting together pieces of information
Interview for a job	117	128	Part 2	groups	30–45	acting out a role play
Jigsaw guessing	37	49	Part 2	groups	5–15	cooperating in working out puzzles
Job prestige	57	71	none	pairs	15–20	ranking jobs
Keep talking	123	132	topic cards	individuals	5–15	delivering a talk
Letters and telegrams	122	132	Part 2	individuals	10–20	condensing a letter into a telegram
Lie detector	21	35	none	groups	10–15	distinguishing between true and false answers
Lifestyle	77	90	objects	pairs	10–15	explaining the significance of objects
Looking for a job	53	67	Part 2	groups	20–40	choosing someone for a job
Mad discussion	59	76	word cards	teams	20–30	defending something

189

Alphabetical table of activities

Activity	No.	Page	Materials	Organisation	Time	Aims/tasks
Magic shop	67	81	word cards	individuals	15–20	bartering human qualities
Making a radio programme	118	128	texts, hardware	groups, pairs class	3–5 hours	writing and recording a radio programme
Messages	110	119	messages	pairs	15–20	miming a message
Messenger	36	48	lego bricks	groups	10–15	giving precise instructions for building something
Miming people and objects	107	116	word cards	individuals, pairs, groups	10–15	guessing mimes
Miracle workers	82	93	Part 2	individuals, groups, class	20–40	thinking about one's aims in life
Most names	20	34	name cards	individuals	15–25	guessing personalities
Name circle	2	14	none	class	5–10	learning names in the class
Names	1	13	paper	class	5–10	finding people
Name tags	3	14	stiff coloured paper, scissors	individuals	10–15	designing name tags
NASA game	51	64	Part 2	individuals, pairs	10–15	ranking objects
New rules	25	37	none	groups	15–25	inventing and guessing rules for a new game
Newspaper report	120	131	photos	groups	20–30	writing a report using certain pictures
One day in London	96	106	none	pairs	15–20	planning a day in London
Opinion poll	15	26	Part 2	groups	30–45	organising an opinion poll
Optimists and pessimists	71	84	none	teams	5–15	making optimistic and pessimistic statements
Ordering	31	44	Part 2	pairs	10–15	ordering the pictures in a comic strip
Our room	97	107	Part 2	pairs	15–20	furnishing a room
Packing a suitcase	19	33	none	class	5–10	guessing people
Partner puzzle	29	43	Part 2	pairs	10–15	following instructions in completing a puzzle
People	72	85	portrait photos	groups	15–25	inventing life stories
Personalities (1)	54	67	list of people	individuals	10–15	choosing a guest speaker
Personalities (2)	76	89	none	individuals, class	10–30	describing people and their influence on one's life
Picture stories	121	131	pictures, cartoon strips	pairs, individuals	15–20	filling in speech bubbles, writing texts
Pink versus brown	68	82	none	groups, pairs	15–25	defending one's preference in colours
PMI	88	97	none	individuals, pairs, class	10–20	evaluating ideas
Priorities	49	62	Part 2	individuals, groups	15–20	ranking statements
Problem page (1)	104	113	Part 2	pairs, groups	20–30	discussing letters and suggesting answers

Activity	No.	Page	Materials	Organisation	Time	Aims/tasks
Problem page (2)	105	**114**	Part 2	individuals, class	20–30	answering letters and discussing them
Qualities	47	**60**	none	individuals, groups, class	10–20	evaluating qualities
Question and answer cards	45	**57**	Part 2	pairs	10–15	asking and answering questions
Question game	40	**53**	Part 2	groups	15–30	answering questions
Rank order	46	**60**	Part 2	individuals	15–20	ranking statements
Rescue	93	**104**	none	groups	10–20	agreeing on criteria for choosing people
Secret topic	60	**77**	none	pairs, class	10–20	discussing a topic without mentioning it
Self-directed interviews	13	**25**	none	pairs	10–30	writing down questions
Shrinking story	63	**79**	Part 2	class	20–30	telling and retelling a story
Similar and different	12	**23**	none	pairs	10–20	discussing similarities and differences
Something else	43	**55**	list of categories	individuals, groups	10–20	listing associations
Something for everybody	99	**109**	none	groups, class	10–20	agreeing on how to spend a sum of money
Spending money	81	**92**	none	individuals, groups	10–25	describing what one would like to buy
Stem sentences	7	**18**	Part 2	individuals	15–20	completing sentences
Strip story	34	**47**	story	class	15–30	reconstructing a text
Swap shop	116	**127**	cards	individuals	20–30	swapping things
Talk show	113	**124**	(hardware)	groups, class	45–90	planning and acting out a talk show
Telephoning	111	**123**	Part 2	pairs	15–20	telephoning with the help of cue cards
Tell us a story	69	**82**	none	groups, class	20–30	telling and analysing a story
The same or different?	27	**41**	Part 2	class, pairs	15–20	describing and comparing pictures
The XY society	115	**126**	none	groups, teams, class	5-8 hours	forming a society
Three adjectives	6	**17**	(word list)	individuals, class	10–15	guessing people
Town plan	32	**44**	Part 2	pairs	10–15	asking for directions on a town plan
Trademark	5	**17**	OHP, transparencies	individuals	15–20	inventing and explaining a trademark
Treasure hunt	98	**108**	tasks	all forms	several days	doing various tasks
TV interview	112	**123**	none	groups	20–30	planning and acting out a TV interview
Twenty things I'd like to do	79	**91**	none	individuals	20–30	listing preferences
Twins	28	**42**	Part 2	pairs	5–10	describing pictures
Unfinished sentences	83	**94**	Part 2	pairs	10–20	completing sentences and discussing them
Uses and abuses	62	**78**	none	teams	10–15	answering nonsense questions

Alphabetical table of activities

Activity	No.	Page	Materials	Organisation	Time	Aims/tasks
Values continuum	80	92	Part 2	individuals, class	15–20	filling in a table and discussing it
Values ladder	52	65	action list	individuals	15–20	ranking actions
Values topics	86	95	Part 2	groups	30	playing a board game
Viewpoints	91	100	Part 2	groups	15–20	planning a role play
Weekend trip	33	45	Part 2	groups	30–45	planning a short holiday
What are the differences?	30	43	Part 2	pairs	5–10	finding differences between pictures
What evidence?	70	83	Part 2	teams, groups	20–30	discussing proof for statements
What is being advertised?	58	75	advertisements	pairs	15–20	guessing advertisements
What is it?	17	32	Part 2	class	5–15	guessing pictures
What's in the box?	23	36	objects in small containers	pairs	10–30	guessing objects
What would happen if . . .?	39	52	situation cards	class	10–15	deciding consequences of events
Which job?	64	80	none	groups	15–20	matching jobs and people, discussing jobs
Word wizard	61	77	none	individuals, pairs	10–15	communicating with very few words (creative writing)

Index to language and level

Language

Adjectives: No. 11
Adverbials of place: Nos. 29, 30, 31, 45, 97
Adverbs: No. 106
Auxiliaries (could, might): Nos. 6, 17, 89
Comparative/superlative: Nos. 47, 89
Comparison: Nos. 54, 67, 68, 93
Conditional: Nos. 19, 43, 64, 87, 90
Future tense (will): No. 65
If-clauses: Nos. 39, 50, 55, 67, 68, 116
-ing form: No. 62
Passive: No. 120
Past continuous: No. 120
Past simple: Nos. 18, 38, 52, 56, 72, 76, 86, 119, 120
Prepositions: Nos. 27, 31, 45
Present perfect: No. 86
Present continuous: Nos. 11, 31
Present simple: Nos. 12, 72, 73, 112
Simple statements: Nos. 2, 5
Word fields: jobs No. 64; colours Nos. 11, 68; appearance/clothes
    No. 11; furniture No. 97

Level

Beginners: Nos. 1–2, 11, 54, 107
Beginners/intermediate: Nos. 8–10, 22, 50, 77, 95, 106, 108,
    119
Intermediate: Nos. 3–7, 12–15, 17–21, 23–25, 27–32, 34–37,
    39–45, 47, 58–59, 61–66, 68–76, 78–92, 96–98, 100–104,
    109–110, 116–117, 120–121
Intermediate/advanced: Nos. 16, 33, 38, 46, 48–49, 51, 53,
    55–57, 67, 93–94, 99, 105, 111–115, 118, 123
Advanced: Nos. 26, 52, 60, 122

Appendix: list of speech acts

Expressing and finding out intellectual and emotional attitudes

expressing one's opinion
I think . . .
I feel that . . .
As far as I'm concerned . . .

asking for someone's opinion
Do you think that . . .?
What do you feel/think about . . .?
Are you sure that . . .?

giving reasons
I think . . . is right because . . .
. . . That's why I feel that . . .
. . . and so I think that . . .

asking for reasons
Why?
Why do you think that . . .?
What makes you feel that . . .?

defending one's opinion
Yes, but what I really mean is . . .
What I'm trying to say is . . .
On the contrary, I . . .
What you said is really an argument for my point of view. I feel . . .

agreeing/supporting other people's opinions
Yes, that's right.
That's what I feel, too.
I think so, too.
Exactly.
I (fully) agree with you.
X put it very well.
I feel that X is right.
X raised some good points.
What X said are the most important . . ., I feel.
OK.

disagreeing/contradicting other people's opinions
I don't agree.
I don't think so.

That's not . . .
You can't say that.
That's no proof.
That's not the point/question/problem . . .
But surely . . .
Oh no, . . .

stating whether something is right or wrong

True.	Wrong.
That's right.	That isn't right.
That's it exactly.	Absolutely not.

expressing certainty and uncertainty, probability and possibility
I'm absolutely certain that . . .
I'm sure that . . .
There is definitely . . .
There may be . . .
Perhaps . . .
. . . might . . .
I'm not at all sure if . . .
. . . could be . . .
I don't think that . . .
. . . is not very likely.
That could/may/might happen.
. . . is not possible.
If A happens X will come.
If A happened X would go.

making comparisons
. . .is not as . . . as . . .
. . . are as . . . as . . .
. . . is a much more important . . . than . . .
. . . are less important than . . .
There are far fewer/not as many arguments for . . . as against . . .
You can't compare . . . with . . .
You have to compare . . . with . . .

making conjectures
C could be a . . .
C looks like . . .
I think/feel that . . .
. . . makes me think of . . .

expressing interest or indifference
I'm interested in . . .
I'd like to know more about . . .
I'd like to do something on . . .
. . . sounds interesting.
Please tell me more about . . .
I'm keen on . . .

. . . doesn't interest me.
I don't care.
What a boring topic.

expressing likes and dislikes
I love/like . . .
. . . is great/very good/fun/fantastic.
I enjoy . . .
What I like best is . . .
I hate/dislike . . .
What I don't like about . . . is . . .
I'm not at all keen on . . .

stating preferences
I'd rather . . .
I prefer . . . to . . .
I'd much rather . . . than . . .

praising
. . . is/are great/wonderful/fantastic/first rate . . .
I've never . . . a better/more interesting/. . . than . . .
. . . is the best . . . I know.
. . . is the most beautiful . . . I've ever seen . . .

expressing intentions
I'm going to . . .
When I'm twenty I'll . . .
In ten years' time I'll . . .
I want to . . .
I intend to . . .

expressing personal insights
I learnt that . . .
It became clear/obvious that . . .
I realised that . . .
I found out about . . .

expressing doubt
I can't say if . . .
I have my doubts about that.
Do you think that . . .? I doubt it.
It's very doubtful whether . . .
You haven't convinced me yet.
You may have a point there, but I'm still not sure . . .
OK, but . . .

Getting things done

asking someone to do something or not to do something
Would you please . . .?
Could you . . .?

Open the . . ., please.
Don't . . .
Stop talking . . .
Never . . .

giving instructions
First put the . . . then . . .
You have to . . . before you can . . .
Let me show you. The . . . goes in here, this . . .
Hold it upright/higher/lower.
Move . . . to the right/left.

expressing understanding
I see.
I've got that.
OK.
That's clear now.
All right.
I didn't hear what you said. Could you speak up, please?
Could you say that again, please.
I didn't understand your last sentence.
Pardon?

asking for confirmation, giving confirmation
. . . Is that what you mean?
Do you want to say . . .?
Did you say that . . .?
You mean that . . ., don't you?
You said . . ., didn't you?
Do we have to fill everything in?
Yes, that's what I meant/wanted to say.

insisting
I have to say again that . . .
I have to insist on . . .
We must keep to the rules.

giving in
All right, then.
OK, you're right.
I take that back.
Perhaps I was a bit too . . .

making suggestions
What about . . .?
We could . . . and then . . .
Let's start with . . .
I suggest that each of us . . .
Why don't we . . .?

complaining
B never says anything.
He/she won't let me see that handout . . .
P talks all the time.
A keeps interrupting/making silly remarks . . .
You're always asking me to write things down/be your speaker . . .

Speech acts for particular situations

role play: assigning roles
Could you act . . ., Peter?
Would you like to be . . ., Peter?
Who'd like to take the part of . . .?
Which part would you like to take, Peter?

asking the way: giving directions
Turn right/left at the next traffic lights.
Walk straight on for . . .
It's the third street on your left/right.
Walk along High Street until you come to . . .

meeting people: introducing someone
This is . . . He's /she's . . .
Sandra, I'd like you to meet . . .

discussions: interrupting
Just a minute . . .
Can I butt in here?
Could you stop here for a moment?
Could I question your last point?
Before you go on, let me . . .

giving evasive answers, hesitating
I'm not sure.
I wouldn't know.
Well, let me think.
I can't say.
Well, . . .

Bibliography

Abbott, E. (1979). 'Communicative exercises: A problem and a suggested solution.' *English Language Teaching Journal* Vol. 33 No. 3, pp. 202–205.

Aronson, E., N. Blaney, J. Sikes, C. Stephan and M. Snapp (1975). 'The jigsaw route to learning and liking.' *Psychology Today* Vol. 8, pp. 43–50.

Black, C. and W. Butzkamm (1977). 'Sprachbezogene und mitteilungsbezogene Kommunikation im Englischunterricht.' *Praxis des neusprachlichen Unterrichts* Vol. 24. No. 2, pp. 115–124.

Brandes, D. and H. Phillips (1979). *Gamester's Handbook: 140 Games for Teachers and Group Leaders*. London: Hutchinson.

Bratt Paulston, C. and H. R. Selekman (1976). 'Interaction activities in the foreign classroom, or how to grow a tulip-rose.' *Foreign Language Annals* Vol. 9 No. 3, pp. 248–254.

British Council (1977). 'Games, simulations and role-playing.' Special Issue of *ELT Documents* (77/1).

Brown, S. and F. Dubin (1975). 'Adapting human relations training techniques for ESL classes.' In Burt and Dulay, 1975, pp. 204–210.

Burt, M. K. and H. C. Dulay (eds.) (1975). *New Directions in Second Language Learning, Teaching and Bilingual Education*. Washington: TESOL.

Byrne, D. (1976). *Teaching Oral English*. London: Longman.

Byrne, D. and S. Rixon (1979). *Communication Games*. ELT Guide 1. London: The British Council.

Byrne, D. and A. Wright (1974). *What Do You Think?* London: Longman.

Chamberlin, A. and K. Stenberg (1976). *Play and Practise!* London: John Murray.

Cole, P. (1970). 'An adaption of group dynamics techniques to foreign language teaching.' *TESOL Quarterly* Vol. 4 No. 4, pp. 353–360.

Davison, A. and P. Gordon (1978). *Games and Simulations in Action*. London: Woburn Press.

de Bono, E. (1973). *CoRT Thinking*. Blandford: Direct Education Services Ltd.

Dixey, J. and M. Rinvolucri (1978). *Get Up and Do It!* London: Longman.

Dobson, J. M. (1974). *Effective Techniques for English Conversation Groups*. Rowley, Mass.: Newbury House.

Dubin, F. and M. Margol (1977). *It's Time to Talk: Communication activities for learning English as a new language*. Englewood Cliffs, New Jersey: Prentice-Hall.

Dubin, F. and E. Olshtain (1977). *Facilitating Language Learning: A Guidebook for the ESL/EFL Teacher*. New York: McGraw-Hill.

Fletcher, M. and J. Buss (1979). *Holiday English Language Programme*. London: Hodder & Stoughton.

Fletcher, M. and D. Birt (1979). *Newsflash!* London: Edward Arnold.

Gibson, R. (1975). 'The strip story: A catalyst for communication.' *TESOL Quarterly* Vol. 9 No. 2, pp. 149–154.

Green, K. (1975). 'Values clarification theory in ESL and bilingual education.' *TESOL Quarterly* Vol. 9 No. 2, pp. 155–164.

Herbert, D and G. Sturtridge (1979). *Simulations*. ELT Guide 2. London: The British Council.

Heyworth, F. (1978). *The Language of Discussion. Role-play exercises for advanced students*. London: Hodder & Stoughton.

Hill, L. A. (1980). *Techniques of Discussion*. London: Evans Bros.

Holden, S. (1981). *Drama in Language Teaching*. London: Longman.

Holden, S. (ed.) (1978). *Visual Aids for Classroom Interaction*. London: Modern English Publications.

Howe, L. W. and M. M. Howe (1975). *Personalizing Education*. New York: Hart.

Johnson, K. and K. Morrow (eds.) (1981). *Communication in the Classroom*. London: Longman.

Jones, K. (1982). *Simulations in Language Teaching*. Cambridge University Press.

Kimball, M. C. and A. S. Palmer (1978). 'The dialog game: A prototypical activity for providing proper intake in formal instruction.' *TESOL Quarterly* Vol. 12 No. 1, pp. 17–29.

Klippel, F. (1980). *Lernspiele im Englischunterricht*. Mit 50 Spielvorschlägen. Paderborn: Schöningh.

Krupar, K. (1973). *Communication Games*. New York: The Free Press.

Learning for Change in World Society (1977). (Compiled by the World Studies Project.) London: One World Trust.

Lee, W. R. (1979). *Language Teaching Games and Contests*. Oxford University Press.

Littlewood, W. (1981). *Communicative Language Teaching*. Cambridge University Press.

Lynch, M. (1977). *It's Your Choice*. London: Edward Arnold.

Maley, A. and A. Duff (1978). *Drama Techniques in Language Learning*. Cambridge University Press (2nd ed. 1982).

McAlpin, J. (1980). *The Magazine Picture Library*. London: Allen & Unwin.

Menné, S. (1975ff). *Q-Cards: Role-playing system for*

conversational English (teaching kits). Tenterden, Kent: Paul Norbury.

Moorwood, H. (ed.) (1978). *Selections from 'Modern English Teacher'*. London: Longman.

Morgenstern, D. (1976). 'Eight activities for the conversation class.' *Modern Language Journal* Vol. 60 Nos. 1–2, pp. 35–38.

Moskowitz, G. (1978). *Caring and Sharing in the Foreign Language Class: A Sourcebook on Humanistic Techniques.* Rowley, Mass.: Newbury House.

Nation, I. S. P. (1977). 'The combining arrangement: Some techniques.' *Modern Language Journal* Vol. 61 Nos. 1–2, pp. 89–94.

Ockenden, M. (1977). *Talking Points*. London: Longman.

Olsen, J. B. (1975). 'ESL communication starters.' In Burt and Dulay 1975, pp. 229–239.

Omaggio, A. (1976). 'Real communication: Speaking a living language.' *Foreign Language Annals* Vol. 9 No. 2, pp. 131–133.

Papalia, A. (1976a). 'From manipulative drills to language for real communication.' *The Canadian Modern Language Review* Vol. 32, pp. 150–155.

Papalia, A. (1976b). *Learner-Centered Language Teaching, Methods and Materials*. Rowley, Mass.: Newbury House.

Puhl, C. A. (1975). 'A practical humanism for developing communicative competence in the ESL learner.' In Burt and Dulay, 1975, pp. 193–203.

Revell, J. (1979). *Teaching Techniques for Communicative English*. London: Macmillan.

Rixon, S. (1981). *How to Use Games in Language Teaching*. London: Macmillan.

Rogers, J. (1978). *Group Activities for Language Learning*. SEAMEO Regional Language Centre Occasional Papers, No. 4. Singapore: SEAMEO Regional Language Centre (MS).

Scarcella, R. C. (1978). 'Socio-drama for social interaction.' *TESOL Quarterly* Vol. 12 No. 1, pp. 41–46.

Seely, J. (1978). *In Role*. London: Edward Arnold.

Simon, S. B., L. W. Howe and H. Kirschenbaum (1972). *Values Clarification*. New York: Hart.

Stanford, G. (1977). *Developing Effective Classroom Groups*. New York: Hart.

Stanford, G. and B. D. Stanford (1969). *Learning Discussion Skills Through Games*. New York: Citation Press.

Syed, H. (1978). 'A classroom project – "The Napoleon Society".' Moorwood (ed.), 1978, pp. 15–17

Taylor, J. L. and R. Walford (1978). *Learning and the Simulation Game*. Milton Keynes: Open University Press. (First published in 1972 by Penguin Books, under the title *Simulation in the Classroom.)*

Thomas, I. (1978). *Communication Activities for Language*

Learning. Wellington: Victoria University, English Language Institute (MS).

Walker, D. (1979). *Dilemmas*. London: Edward Arnold.

Wright, A. (1976). *Visual Materials for the Language Teacher*. London: Longman.

Wright, A. D. Betteridge and M. Buckby (1979). *Games for Language Learning*. Cambridge University Press (2nd ed. 1984).

Zelson, S. N. J. (1974). 'Skill-using activities in the foreign language classroom.' *American Foreign Language Teacher* Vol. 4 No. 3, pp. 33–35.